New
Beginnings

OTHER BOOKS BY LIONEL WHISTON

Are You Fun to Live With?
Enjoy the Journey
Power of a New Life: Relational Studies in Mark
Through Suffering to Victory: Relational Studies in Mark

Lionel Whiston

New Beginnings

Relational Studies in
Mark

WORD BOOKS, Publisher, Waco, Texas

First Printing, January 1976
Second Printing, March 1976

Unless otherwise credited, all Scripture quotations are from The Revised Standard Version, copyrighted 1946 (renewed 1973), 1956, and © 1971 by the Division of Christian Education of the National Council of the Churches of Christ in the U.S.A. and are used by permission.

The quotation credited to Phillips is from *The New Testament in Modern English* by J. B. Phillips, © 1958, 1960, 1972, by J. B. Phillips and published by The Macmillan Company.

The quotation credited to Berkeley is from The Berkeley Version of the Bible, copyright 1958, 1959 by Zondervan Publishing House.

Quotations marked NEB are from *The New English Bible* © The Delegates of The Oxford University Press and The Syndics of The Cambridge University Press, 1961, 1970, and are used by permission.

The quotation credited to Moffatt is from James Moffatt, *The Bible, a New Translation,* copyright 1922, 1924, 1926, 1935 by Harper & Brothers.

The quotation credited to Goodspeed is from *The Bible: An American Translation,* copyright 1935 by the University of Chicago Press.

The quotation marked LB is from *The Living Bible, Paraphrased,* copyright 1971 by Tyndale House Publishers, and is used by permission of the publisher.

CONTENTS

INTRODUCTION

The Bible comes alive for me as I imagine myself in the place of the various persons and situations in its stories. That is what I would like to do in this series of three books—to compare our own inner lives with the biblical narratives and, by evaluating them in that light, to discover direction and meaning for our living in the contemporary scene.

I have written these studies for those within the Christian tradition. While they are primarily for study groups they may be used for personal study or devotions.

Mark's Gospel portrayed Jesus as the Son of God, Savior and Sovereign of the world, who by his mighty works demonstrated God's unlimited power and grace, and who by his death and resurrection revealed God to be the Giver of victory over sin and death. Jesus was revealed as God's "Man for others" and as "God for us." Emphasis is placed on Jesus' avowed purpose to change, by his teaching and life, the concept of the long anticipated Messiah.

New Beginnings covers Mark 1 through 4:34, ending with a series of parables. *Power of a New Life* begins with 4:35 and a series of miracles around the Sea of Galilee, and ends at 9:50 with Jesus on the way to Jeru-

salem. *Through Suffering to Victory* goes from Mark 10:1
through 16:8, covering the end of Jesus' ministry, his
suffering, death and resurrection. I have omitted 16:
9–20, since the most ancient manuscripts do not have
these verses which are thought to have been added in the
second century.

In going through Mark, I have followed the major
divisions outlined by *The Interpreter's Bible* (vol. 7,
p. 636). Each study consists of three parts: a Scripture
passage (using the Revised Standard Version), com-
ments, and questions. The question sections are detailed
at length to help readers do their own thinking. Many
questions will not yield a ready answer but are such as
need to be lived with.

Since the purpose of these studies is slanted toward
relational living, little has been said about historical and
social backgrounds, theological implications, biblical
scholarship and criticism, important as these are. Rather
we have sought to explore Jesus' relationship to himself,
his Father and his fellow men, and then consider the
same parallel threefold relationship in our own lives.

While I have largely drawn on my own experience of
many years in the ministry, I am indebted for many
seminal thoughts to Dr. Frederick C. Grant, who wrote
on Mark in *The Interpreter's Bible* (vol. 7) and to Dr.
Eduard Schweizer, *The Good News According to Mark*
(Atlanta: John Knox Press, 1970).

I wish to express appreciation to Phyllis Amidon,
George and Joyce Adam and Marilyn Hardy, who have
used parts of the manuscript in group study, and to
Priscilla Houghton, all of whom have made valuable com-

ments. My son, Dr. Lionel A. Whiston, Jr., of Eden Theological Seminary, has given me the benefit of his rich scholarship and insight. My wife has been a constant inspiration as well as making valued contributions to the book.

ABOUT THIS VOLUME

New Beginnings follows Jesus as he walked the pathways of Galilee, healing, caring, loving—bringing wholeness of mind and body. He challenged the time-worn traditions of the Pharisees, announcing that the Kingdom of God is with us now. Thus the power of God, through Jesus, entered history, giving victory over evil and sickness, and ushering humanity into a new age of hope and dignity. Jesus offered to all fellowship and growing fulfillment in his Kingdom. The verdict still stands, "We never saw anything like this."

OUTLINE OF MARK

Volume I   New Beginnings (1–4:34)
  Introduction 1:1–13
  Jesus about the Sea of Galilee 1:13–4:34
    Miracles of healing
    Calling and training of the disciples
    The beginnings of controversy with the Pharisees
    Teachings about the nature of the Kingdom
Volume II   Power of a New Life (4:35–9:50)
  Jesus, by the Sea of Galilee and Wider Journeyings
    Jesus, Lord of life and nature
    More miracles of healing
    The death of John the Baptist
    The tradition of the elders
    The feeding of the multitudes
    Deepening controversy with the Pharisees
    Peter's confession
    The transfiguration and the epileptic boy
Volume III   Through Suffering to Victory (10:1–16:8)
  Jesus in Jerusalem
    Incidents on the way to Jerusalem
    The apocalyptic discourse
    The passion story
    The empty tomb, "He is alive"!

Adapted from *The Interpreter's Bible,* vol. 7, p. 636.

1.
GOD INVADES HISTORY

Mark 1:1–3

(1) The beginning of the gospel of Jesus Christ, the Son of God.

(2) As it is written in Isaiah the prophet, "Behold, I send my messenger before thy face, who shall prepare thy way; (3) the voice of one crying in the wilderness: Prepare the way of the Lord, make his paths straight—"

Verse 1: This verse serves as a title for the Gospel. Beginnings are where hope is born, where dreams and newness break through into life. Life begins in Christ and yet "continues to begin." We have been created, but are constantly, under Christ, being re-created. And so life is a series of "recommencements." God through Christ is a constant source of creativity and newness.

The Gospel [Good News] of Jesus Christ: This is the Good News that God has come to earth in Jesus, that through him we have a pathway to salvation and well-being. It is bad news to those who find his way too costly and reject him. At any moment we can choose emerging life or waning death.

This Good News began in the world at a point of time in history two thousand years ago. Our very automobile number plates declare that God divided time into a

11

cosmic before and after. It is also Good News for us now the moment we trust in Jesus Christ. It continues to be Good News and have freshness and newness as we renew our fellowship with and our obedience to him.

The Son of God: To the Jew this meant the Messiah, the long-awaited and hoped-for One. To Christendom, he is God in the flesh, God made available: He is God with a face!

Verse 2: When the prophet said these words, Israel was in captivity. Those were discouraging and lonely years for Israel. In such a time a messenger came announcing the coming of their Lord. So often when the children of Israel had nearly abandoned hope, God sent reassurance of help and deliverance. This experience is the basis of the old folk saying, "It is always darkest just before the dawn." God is at work even when he is most invisible! God's coming is always imminent. If only our faith would be strong enough to make us aware of this! Life in Christ is always pregnant with hope.

Verse 3: God needs messengers to announce his coming, but these messengers must be the embodiment of their message, people who will do the spade work of preparation—prepare the way, straighten the path. The work of surveyors and construction crews precedes the completion of highways and the joys of travel.

QUESTIONS

Verse 1: Is Jesus only an interesting historical personage to you? Admirable? How is he different from other historic VIPs: Luther, Lincoln, etc.? How is the Good News in present day-by-day living becoming new and real?

Is the presence of Christ in your life always Good News? Or does he make you very uncomfortable? Is this discomfort prelude to new growth or to discouragement? Is he both Judge and Savior? Does encounter with Christ comfort you or challenge you—or both? Which of these responses needs to be strengthened?

Describe in what ways the Good News of Jesus Christ brings hope into your life and into your situation.

Verse 2: When you enter the home, the office or any meeting, are you "good news" or "bad news"? Does your presence bring joy or uptightness where you go? In a time of despair the prophet brought a message of hope. Is your life style, your daily moods and attitudes, a herald of the good things ahead? Can you sing when life is bleak?

Verse 3: Do you see yourself so loving people that your very presence seems to bring them closer to God and the realities of life? Recall an instance when loving listening, patience and friendship have been a prelude to the entrance of the spirit of Christ into your life or your friend's or both.

Do you feel you must be "the whole show" or are you willing to be the "forerunner" and let someone else, through God's Spirit, complete the work? What spadework (cf. construction gangs on a road) is necessary in your life if you are to prepare a highway for the Lord's entry into your home, job or church? What crooked ways need to be straightened? What relationships in your life need healing? Be specific.

Think of the cost of building a highway, straightening a bad curve, building an overpass today. It costs more when civilization has settled in around these highways. Work out parallels of the need and cost of reconstruction in your life now that the habit patterns of the years have settled in on your life and behavior, now that contemporary civilization has corroded the spiritual attitudes and behavior of our times. Where and how can you begin in your own life? What demolition must take place? Excavation? Foundation and support? Fill? Smooth surfacing?

2.
HE POINTED TO THE CHRIST

Mark 1:4–8

(4) John the baptizer appeared in the wilderness, preaching a baptism of repentance for the forgiveness of sins. (5) And there went out to him all the country of Judea, and all the people of Jerusalem; and they were baptized by him in the river Jordan, confessing their sins. (6) Now John was clothed with camel's hair, and had a leather girdle around his waist, and ate locusts and wild honey. (7) And he preached, saying, "After me comes he who is mightier than I, the thong of whose sandals I am not worthy to stoop down and untie. (8) I have baptized you with water; but he will baptize you with the Holy Spirit."

Verses 4–6: As a foghorn warns a sailor of hidden rocks, John warned of pitfalls and sins. A stern, desert-reared ascetic, he thundered the words of God. He blasted his way through the hypocrisy and false piety of the day. His emphasis was on repentance and baptism.

This message has its limitations. It is not enough to instill fear, even though it leads to repentance and baptism. John recognized this and he spoke of Jesus completing the task with the baptism of the Holy Spirit.

We are all called to be forerunners of Jesus. Some of us are stern, some are wooers and lovers. There is the surgeon's knife and the nurse's loving care, the medicines of man and the healing processes of God. All are included in the bringing of wholeness. John thundered against the sins of his hearers. There are times for such messages. There are also times to lead men into the broad expanses of effective living. A Mississippi River pilot was asked if he knew where all the shoals lay. "No," he said, "but I know where the deep water is."

Verses 7–8: How often as a preacher my ministry pointed to myself; I mused, "Do my people like me?" "Did they like my sermon?" "Many people spoke to me today. It must have been a good message"! But John did not look for glory for himself. He pointed to the Christ.

QUESTIONS

Verse 4: The desert may have made John stern and hard. Does your environment determine your outlook and behavior? Is it tempered by God's love? Conversely, has a comfortable home or today's sensate, suburban culture dulled the sensitivity and cutting edge of your compassion for others less fortunate? Think about this.

Verse 5: Is your life largely based on a one-time repentance or on a series of repentances, or both? Is it also based on the indwelling Christ leading to growth and maturity? Are you forever being forgiven and only this? Or are you exploring new fields of growth, service and adventure with Christ? Do you believe it is possible to achieve a spiritual goal once and for all? Note Peter's phrase, "Grow up to salvation" (1 Pet. 2:2). Are recommitments necessary? Helpful? Are we always subject to the frailties of our humanity?

Verses 7–8: In what way do you see yourself as a fore-runner of Jesus? Does your life style as friend, parent, spouse, employer, employee make it more likely that the Spirit of Jesus will enter the lives of those next to you?

Do you tend to take the glory of life to yourself? Does your life tend to reflect credit on you or on him? How often do you want people to know the amount of money you give or subtly wish they could learn of it without your telling? How about your good works? Is it important to you who gets the credit for your deeds? Your ideas?

When someone else gets the credit for something you have done, how eager are you that people should know the real facts? Do you "sweetly" refrain, but really want to tell? Do you have an inner feeling of smugness?

Discuss your baptism: what it meant if baptized in adulthood, or what the Sacrament means to you now as you reflect on the significance of your baptism as an infant and your reaffirmation of the baptismal vows when you joined the church. What are your inner thoughts and feelings as you witness the baptism of others? Baptism by water signifies repentance, forgiveness and cleansing. Is continuance of repentance necessary? As you grow in sensitivity and awareness, are new sins revealed? Are there also new infillings of the Spirit, closer walks with man and God? Speak of this.

3.
GOD SAYS, "YOU'RE O.K."

Mark 1:9–11
(9) In those days Jesus came from Nazareth of Galilee and was baptized by John in the Jordan. (10) And when he came up out of the water, immediately he saw the heavens opened and the Spirit descending upon him like a dove; (11) and a voice came from heaven, "Thou art my beloved Son; with thee I am well pleased."

Verse 9: The sentence, "In those days Jesus came from Nazareth" reminds us that Jesus is a historic figure, living in the current situations of his time. He who was to "become sin for our sakes," asked for the rite of baptism, a symbol of dying and rising. Jesus' act was followed by God's reassuring voice. It is *after* and not *before* our obedience to him that we feel the presence and benediction of God. We have to risk moving out in faith, in "fear and trembling." But after having been obedient, then comes the blessing! (Cf. Luke 17:14.)

Verse 10: Like a dove. Jewish thinking tended to be symbolic. To picture a dove in this scene literally alighting on Jesus' head is to miss the inwardness of this passage, just as to see a big spread of feathers held over our heads would be to miss the beauty of "He shall cover thee with his feathers" (Ps. 91:4a, KJV). One translation

(Berkeley) has it, "And the Spirit, dovelike, descended."

Verse 11: I recall reading this verse some years ago, and the words suddenly leaped out of the page and became *real for me.* I had never felt loved as a child. My father always held before me the perfect goal which I never attained; thus I felt I had not earned his favor. He saw my faults and I felt he was displeased with me. Unwittingly I transferred this feeling to God. He too, I thought, was demanding perfection of me, keeping his "black book" and recording all my misdeeds. I never could do enough "good deeds" to balance accounts. My life's endeavors were always "in the red."

This day as I read this verse I knew deep in my heart that God was saying to me, *"Lee Whiston, you are my beloved son in whom I am well pleased."* He was really speaking to me! His love and favor toward me were not dependent on my good behavior. God really loved me just as I was. I had become a favored son of his—as indeed all of us can become. It set me free to enjoy God and to receive his love and his life. I became the recipient of his unmerited love and favor!

QUESTIONS

Verse 9: Have you accepted the fact that your life is to be lived in the here-and-now situation? Do you find a tendency to live in "if only" land? With fantasies and unreality? If we cannot love and serve where we are, we certainly cannot where we are not. How many experiences are unfulfilled in your life because you postpone attempts by an attitude of "When this or that happens, I'll take action"?

If Jesus had had any false pride, he would not have submitted to baptism by John. Does pride keep you from some of God's blessings? Is the making of new friends denied you because of your unwillingness to associate with people whose behavior differs from yours and that of your friends? Are the wisdom and insights of many books closed to you because you differ with their points of view and feel in full possession of the truth?

Verse 10: Do you always wait for a sense of certainty before acting? Tell of some instance where you were fearful and uncertain and yet felt impelled to act? Describe your feelings following the act of obedience. What happened to the fear? Did it dissolve? Decrease? Remain?

God is eager to give you his Spirit and to affirm you by calling you his son, his daughter, as he did with Jesus. What steps are you taking to receive God's affirmation and love? You are really very special to him! Do you believe he is saying to you, "You're O.K."? As a result, can you say of yourself, "I'm O.K."?

4.
TEMPTED AS WE ARE

> *Mark 1:12–13*
> (12) The Spirit immediately drove him out into the
> wilderness. (13) And he was in the wilderness forty days,
> tempted by Satan; and he was with the wild beasts; and
> the angels ministered to him.

It is a law of life that spiritual "highs" are followed
by spiritual "lows." After the victory on Mt. Carmel,
Elijah fled from the threats of Jezebel, saying "Lord, take
away my life; for I am no better than my fathers" (1 Kings
19:4). Jesus' experience of baptism was followed by a
temptation as threatening as the baptism was blessed.

The number *forty* does not only refer to the exact
number of days but to the completeness of the temptation, even as the account of forty years in the wilderness
symbolized the thoroughness of the testing and discipline
imposed on the children of Israel. In the desert, they
found identity and a sense of purpose. Jesus, for his part,
affirmed his Messiahship and sharpened his sense of mission and willingness to obey his Father.

Temptation has meaning for man only because he is
free to yield or resist. Freedom of will implies the inevitability of temptation. Jesus had no magic power to resist
it or his victory would have no helpfulness for you or

me in our own humanness. He could have yielded, but he did not.

The wild beasts and angels symbolize the opposing forces that surrounded Jesus. Again we observe the Hebrew love of symbols to express hidden spiritual powers. This temptation must be seen as something very real and very costly if Jesus' example is to mean anything to us.

Immediately following periods of spiritual elation such as Christmas, Easter, or a new commitment, I find that for me there follow times of severe temptation. Overprograming myself or the giving of myself extensively to serve others without taking proper time for rest opens the door for discouragement and temptation.

I find that Satan tempts me at the points of my strength rather than my weakness. I am aware of my weakness and more apt to turn to Christ for help. Among my strengths are love and generosity. So I am tempted to be sentimental, possessive or directive in my love. I am tempted to be lustful or indulgent to myself (feeling I have the right to a "moral holiday" after having faithfully served God for a while!) and/or indulgent to others. I will sentimentally try to help people rather than helping them to help themselves. The Napoleonic strategy was to strike at the enemy's strength. My strengths are the targets for the evil that would attack me.

QUESTIONS

Do your temptations come at stated times? When is this? Can you prepare for them and bolster against them?

Do you have spiritual "money in the bank" in readiness?

Where and under what circumstances are you tempted? Is there a recurring pattern? What can you do about it?

Do you see God's plan behind temptations? What benefits come from temptations? When you give in? When you are victorious?

What are some of your strengths? Do you recognize the temptations that come in these areas? Describe some. What steps do you take to bring victory?

Have you tried thanking God when you are tempted? Such as, "Thank you, God, for this temptation. It is too much for me. It drives me to you and in you I find strength and victory." Does this attitude help? What meaning do you discover in the request in the Lord's Prayer, "Lead us *not* into temptation"?

What does the fact that Jesus was severely tempted suggest about the relationship of God and Jesus? What kind of feelings do you think were in the heart of God as his son was being tempted? Do you believe he has similar feelings when you are tempted?

Should parents allow their children to be tempted? If so, to what degree? What would happen if all temptations were taken away? What principles are to be observed regarding parents letting children be tempted?

5.
THE FOURFOLD ANNOUNCEMENT

Mark 1:14–15

(14) Now after John was arrested, Jesus came into Galilee, preaching the gospel of God, (15) and saying, "The time is fulfilled, and the kingdom of God is at hand; repent, and believe in the gospel."

Verse 15: The time is fulfilled: The word *time* does not refer to a particular year or month, but rather to the timing of God, the fulfilling of his purposes, the ripeness of the situation. There is always a sense of rightness about God's timing. A friend writes, "When I do things in God's timing and not my own, things flow smoothly, doors open, hearts and minds receive rather than reject." To synchronize our living with his timing is to sense his purposes and to move in on the flood of the Holy Spirit's power. Today the Master is still saying to us, "The time is fulfilled. This is my moment for you to be, to live and to become as never before."

The kingdom of God is at hand: To the Jews this declaration meant that the long-awaited Messiah was here. No wonder they could not see in this humble carpenter their king whom they expected to throw down their enemies and rule with power. To the disciples it was to mean that the Kingdom of God—a new life style—was personified and incarnated in Jesus right there and then. It took a long time for them to realize this.

To Christendom, Jesus' declaration means that the "now moment" is always potentially "God's moment." Each moment, we can live and move within his love. The outer facts of life may seem to deny the presence of God's Kingdom in the world, but his Kingdom may always be within us and therefore always at hand. Every moment may be one in which to realize his presence and to live and move in him. The indwelling Christ personifies this Kingdom. He and the Kingdom are both within us—a present reality.

Repent: This is a call to change our attitudes, to face the fact of sin in ourselves and to reverse the direction of our lives. The disciples revised their ideas about the character of the Messiah, their attitude toward the Romans, toward each other—in fact toward all of personal relationships. Repentance means not merely being sorry for our past life styles, but being sorry enough to quit the old way and begin a new life style modeled for us by Jesus. Without such a complete changeover in our attitudes and patterns of behavior, our repentance would be emasculated into mere regret or remorse. True repentance leads to new attitudes of heart, new depths of commitment, new styles of relationships, new ways of living, and new creative interaction on the frontiers of need, poverty, racism and war.

Believe in the gospel—Good News: The call to believe is a call to faith. It asks that the Good News may claim the center of our attention and priority in our loyalties. The media spew out the evils of our day, happenings from the remote corners of the world down to our very doorsteps. Our next-door neighbor or fellow committee member spreads ugly rumor in the form of gossip. We live in a world of bad news!

Here is a call to hear God's Good News of Jesus Christ amid the world's cries of turmoil and evil, to believe in the good, and the coming of the Kingdom of God in spite of the appearances around us, and so to set our loyalties that we respond affirmatively to the goodness of God rather than react negatively to the presence of evil. The psalmist wrote, "I believe that I shall see the goodness of the Lord in the land of the living" (Ps. 27:13).

QUESTIONS

The time is fulfilled: Can you tell of one incident when you sought to achieve something when the time was not ripe? When you did it in your time and not God's? Spell out the difference between your time and God's time. Note Jesus' words, "My time has not yet come, but your time is always here" (John 7:6). Tell how you are seeking to live according to God's timing. Are your days lived in expectancy? Is life on tiptoe because each day is fulfilled (filled full) by God's presence and purposes?

The kingdom of God is both within you and yet to come in the world. But the Kingdom is also in the process of "becoming" both in you and in the world. Talk about how you feel and believe the Kingdom to be growing, both within you and around you.

Christ is already here. He has come. Do not let the hope for a distant Second Coming diminish the glory and power of his already present arrival. Are you actually living as if he were here? He is, you know!

Repent: Repentance is a first-time "happening" and then a continuing process. Astronauts speak of mid-course correctives. Tell of your initial repentance, and then of some subsequent "correctives."

In what ways has repentance been for you a change in attitudes, moods and behavior? Tell of a time when you were not sorry enough to change your attitudes or behavior so that what might have been repentance was only sorrow and remorse.

Believe means "be-live," "live by," or "trust in." Does the Good News of Christ set your mood for the day—or does your cup of coffee, the newspaper headlines or the weather? In other words, what do you really live by? Is this the way you really want it?

Belief involves thinking, willing and acting. Are you hung up on any of these? When you think of Jesus, does it challenge your intellect and satisfy your intelligence that his way of life is realistic and ultimately the only way of life that will work? Are you seeking to be so committed to his life style that the inner fiber of your being responds to him? Are you seeking to act out his life style in your daily life? Speak of this and of how you can obey the command, "Believe in the gospel."

Which kind of news are you spreading? Bad News: rumor, gossip, the faults, sins and crimes of our day, the discouraging and pessimistic moods of the times? Or Good News: dreams, aspirations, the signs of hope in the world, the hidden potentials in people, faith in life, in people and in God's ultimate triumph?

6.
UNQUESTIONING OBEDIENCE

Mark 1:16–20

(16) And passing along by the Sea of Galilee, he saw Simon and Andrew the brother of Simon casting a net in the sea; for they were fishermen. (17) And Jesus said to them, "Follow me and I will make you become fishers of men." (18) And immediately they left their nets and followed him. (19) And going on a little farther, he saw James the son of Zebedee and John his brother, who were in their boat mending the nets. (20) And immediately he called them; and they left their father Zebedee in the boat with the hired servants, and followed him.

Verse 16: Passing—the act of walking (or driving) can be merely to get somewhere, wasted time between two engagements! Recently I found myself hurrying to the post office, a two-block walk. The journey was something to be put behind me so I could get back to work again. Suddenly I thought, "I'm not on an errand to the post office. I'm walking with God." My shoulders straightened, I started singing quietly, I was in his presence—life was suddenly beautiful. Incidentally, I still was going to the post office! All of life can have overtones of heaven!

When we are in such a mood we often see people or

landmarks that would otherwise have gone unnoticed. Jesus saw Simon and Andrew.

Verse 17: He called them to follow him. As they obeyed, their lives were lifted into a new dimension. They were to be not merely fishers of fish, but fishers of men. An employer said, "Before I knew Christ I was turning out a product. Since then a new relationship between employer and employees has developed throughout our plant that enables us to turn out men!" A woman expressed it, "I've been changed from a housekeeper to a homemaker." Another, "I am now a spiritual as well as a biological parent." Customers become persons, congregations become individuals with deep needs, fellow motorists are seen as children of God.

Verses 18–20: The word *immediately,* frequently used by Mark in the Gospel, occurs twice in this passage, once in connection with Simon and Andrew's response to Jesus, and again with Jesus' response to the inner leading of the Spirit that he should call James and John.

Prompt obedience to God's will adds joy to the task. I can easily lie in bed when I know I should get up, or delay starting a job, or listen to TV when some task waits to be done. The very slowness of my obedience robs me of part of the joy it might bring.

These disciples left behind what in all likelihood were lucrative and exciting tasks. How often God calls us to leave behind the good in order that we may receive the best. To hold on to old patterns of thought, habits of action, molds of behavior closes the doors to the new and exciting discoveries, life styles, and freedoms that he would offer to us.

QUESTIONS

Verse 16: When you travel from place to place—a short walk down a corridor to an office or a one-hundred-mile drive—are you enjoying the walk, the fellowship of the Master and/or of people, or are you straining and pushing so as not to lose time? Are you worrying about the errand's outcome? Think and talk of this. What do you see when you drive—cars and a highway, or the miracles and handiwork of God and man? Tell of your experiences.

Verse 17: Follow me. Is your religion mostly an ethic, a behavioral pattern, an attempt at perfectionism? Or is it a relationship, a walking with a Friend, Jesus Christ? The former tends to produce pressure, a desire to "measure up." The latter issues in a joyous, relaxed way of life. Discuss these two ways of living.

Does the behavioral pattern still linger? Can you move ever farther into joyous companionship with Jesus Christ? Note the word *become*. It suggests continuing action. It points to natural growth rather than straining and forced growth. Which growth is characteristic of you?

Tell how your fellowship with Christ has lifted life into a new dimension—at home, school, job, church and/or community.

Verses 18–20: All four disciples *left* things and people behind. What and who have you left? What does it mean to leave someone for Christ's sake? See Matthew 10:37–39. What and/or who is God still asking you to leave behind and in what way? What choices are you called upon to make in order to follow God's plan for your life? What do Christ's words "Follow me" ask of you today?

Does the promptness of your obedience vary? When are you most apt to be quick and joyous in response to God's will? When tardy and reluctant? What does this tell you about yourself? Do childhood patterns play a part here?

7.
JESUS CONFRONTS EVIL

Mark 1:21–28

(21) And they went into Capernaum; and immediately on the sabbath he entered the synagogue and taught. (22) And they were astonished at his teaching, for he taught them as one who had authority, and not as the scribes. (23) And immediately there was in their synagogue a man with an unclean spirit; (24) and he cried out, "What have you to do with us, Jesus of Nazareth? Have you come to destroy us? I know who you are, the Holy One of God." (25) But Jesus rebuked him, saying, "Be silent, and come out of him!" (26) And the unclean spirit, convulsing him and crying with a loud voice, came out of him. (27) And they were all amazed, so that they questioned among themselves, saying, "What is this? A new teaching! With authority he commands even the unclean spirits, and they obey him." (28) And at once his fame spread everywhere throughout all the surrounding region of Galilee.

Verse 21: It was Jesus' habit to go to the synagogue, but it was not habitual. There is a difference. When things become habitual, the freshness is lost. Jesus had a sense of adventure as he went to the temple.

Verse 22: When Jesus arose and took part in the public service, his authority did not stem from a heavy-handed laying down of the law. Rather he spoke of the realities of life in a way that related deeply to people. This was true of all of his contacts with people. The Samaritan woman said, "Come, see a man who told me all that I ever did" (John 4:29). Jesus revealed people to themselves. What he said plumbed the depths of their beings and authenticated itself. They knew he was speaking the truth.

Verses 23–24: The forces of evil also recognize the truth. In the face of the very apparent truth and righteousness of Jesus, evil could not remain unmoved. It had either to slink away, or stand up and resist. It is the nature of evil to hate the good. Iago says of Othello, "He hath a daily beauty in his life that makes me ugly."

How often we see the advent of Jesus as threatening or even destructive. At one period of my ministry on occasion I "stole" sermons, preaching them without giving credit and passing them off as my own. To deprive me of the crutch of stolen sermons was threatening.

There was a time when I depended far more on hard work and on Lee Whiston's abilities than on God's Spirit to work in other people's lives. When God faced me with the alternative of doing his will in a relaxed and orderly manner, rather than my frenzied attempts to accomplish more and more work each day, my heart sank at the prospect of unfinished tasks and a sagging church program. For God to challenge my self-centered egotistic way of running my church seemed to threaten me with utter ruin. It would be my very undoing!

However, evil and selfish ways are false crutches that eventually weaken and destroy a person. Christ is not our undoing, but our hope. Sin's false foundation is replaced with his sure foundation.

Verse 25: This tender Man who held children on his knee could also be stern and strong. He could confront evil in whatever form. He was not afraid of sin or sinners. We Christians need this inner strength for rugged encounter. I sometimes quail before evil, rather than stand up to it.

Verse 26: I do not understand very much about unclean spirits, demons and demonology, but I do know when evil possesses me. I recognize it in others. And of this I am certain: I know that Christ has power over the evil in me whenever I turn to him. I know that often he helps me to bring victory to the evil-possessed. Sometimes it takes place at once, sometimes it requires weeks or years to happen. Sometimes it does not happen. But I continue on in faith believing that Christ is the answer and holds ultimate power for all persons and all situations.

A man plagued by fears and evil desire sought me out for counseling. God led me to grasp his hands and tell him that deep in his life lay the untapped reservoir of God's love, in whose image he was made. I told him that together through Christ we could at that moment claim God's victorious love in his life and the defeat of fear and evil. Tears flowed freely, a new light came in his eyes. We knelt to claim God's forgiveness and inflowing strength. A man had been set free and embarked on a new way of life.

Verse 27: Jesus' contemporaries wondered if this was a new teaching. No, it was not a new teaching. It was the embodiment of these teachings by Jesus that was new.

He lived them! The Word was made flesh. The power of God in Jesus' flesh was greater than the power of evil incarnate in others.

There is always the question as to whether we should speak to other people about their sins. It is often necessary to enter into a warm relationship with others before speaking; indeed, to earn by deep love the right to speak. Sam Shoemaker used to say, "Don't trouble about the other fellow's sins until they trouble him. Meanwhile, surround him with a life of love in the Spirit, until he begins to be restless and seeking."

QUESTIONS

Verse 21: What religious habits (church attendance, prayer, grace at table, Bible reading, etc.) have become habitual for you and therefore lost much meaning or power? Do you expect anything to happen when you go to church, when you pray, or read the Bible? What can you do about this? Should you continue with a habit that has lost its meaning? What can you do to restore meaning?

Verse 22: When you talk do you tend to pull rank, strive for one-upmanship, try to be right, play games, or do you speak of those deeper inner realities that validate themselves? Are you "for real," speaking from the place where you really are? Do you talk from idea levels or feeling levels? Think about this and talk it over.

Have your words lost their power? Why? Has someone ever said to you, "Oh, I've heard you say that a hundred times"? Or do you speak of what you have discovered through experience? Do your words have authority and freshness because they are real?

Verses 23–28: What do you do in the face of evil? In yourself? In others? Stand or run? Do you recognize the inherent weakness of evil? Do you feel the strength of God in and through you to overcome it? Tell of incidents where you have faced or failed to face evil in yourself, and in another. What happened? When should you face another person with his sin? When be silent? In this Scripture the man openly challenged Jesus. This opened the door for Jesus to speak. Note that Jesus did not *argue,* he commanded. In what way do you face evil? Do you argue? Or claim the authority of Jesus and the victorious power of the Holy Spirit? Instead of arguing, can you speak of an example of God's power and then leave this witness for the Spirit of God to use?

8.
THE MASTER'S REENTRY

Mark 1:29–31
(29) And immediately he left the synagogue, and entered the house of Simon and Andrew, with James and John. (30) Now Simon's mother-in-law lay sick with a fever, and immediately they told him of her. (31) And he came and took her by the hand and lifted her up, and the fever left her; and she served them.

Verse 29: Here is that word *immediately* again. It does not convey hurry or frenzy as is so often true of us, but rather a sense of purpose, a prompt response to need, to the doing of God's will. Jesus had encountered the man with the unclean spirit. He was undoubtedly spent and empty. We read later (5:30) that healing drained power from him. Yet even though he had had a difficult and trying day, he did not come home to seek rest and protection from the demands of people. He was not a nine-to-five person. He was ready to respond to the need of this feverish woman.

Verse 30: Was this woman's fever psychosomatic? Was she frightened at the thought of entertaining this miracle worker and his band of followers? Peter had left his fishing. Could she have been resentful towards Jesus for taking away a source of her income? All this was more than enough to cause a fever! We do not know if there was a previous acquaintance, whether Jesus talked to Simon's mother-in-law first or prayed before he touched her. We may be sure he prayed inwardly to his Father.

Verse 31: What a warm, reassuring touch Jesus must have had! How gently and yet how firmly he must have lifted her! The miracle happened; the fever was gone. She was well and able to prepare the meal for the hungry men.

Many of us are unaware that we have a gift for bringing health and well-being to others. I was over fifty years of age before I realized that silently holding someone's hand and believing that God's power was flowing through me to him could be the means of bringing wholeness to someone. Try it with a sick child, a mate while he or she sleeps, or with a friend.

I have, on occasion, been sick and running a temperature. Just the presence of our doctor, an old-time, much-loved friend, has calmed my fears and lessened the fever, even without medicine or therapy. How much more could this happen when Jesus entered the room with his calm assurance exuding peace and confidence to everyone and his power flowing into another's life.

The closing four words are, "and she served them." Her service to them is evidence of a thorough healing, body and mind. She does not pamper herself, fearful she may be sick again, but steps into the kitchen in faith to prepare a meal and wait on them. There must have been great gratitude in her heart not only for her own healing, but for the change in her son-in-law Simon, since he had been associated with Jesus.

Let us look at her service from Jesus' point of view. He was tired. He might well have wanted to go off to rest. He might have chosen to have a lesser meal than her deep gratitude prompted her to serve. Yet he received her service graciously. He knew her need to express thanks and hence his responsibility to receive her gratitude.

A friend of mine wrote, "After an illness, one of the hardest things I have had to learn was to let my husband wait on me. I've always been very self-sufficient. My lesson in humility was to see the job done by another—differently than I would do it—but to come to realize it was sometimes done better than I would have done it. What a joy to find that after a while Jesus freed me so that I couldn't even remember how I originally had done the job!"

QUESTIONS

Does the genial atmosphere you experienced at church disappear if you come home and find some trouble? Recall incidents such as losing your patience or temper before church because the children are not ready, losing it again when you come home to find the meat burned, a child disobedient, or someone sick.

When you have been away—shopping, at work or on a pleasure jaunt—does coming home pose a reentry problem? Are you ready to serve when you might feel you have a right to rest? (See Phil. 4:13: "I am ready for anything through the strength of the one who lives within me," Phillips.)

When you face a situation where another is in need, can you humbly, and yet confidently, feel a sense of power in yourself, even as Jesus when he took the woman's hand and lifted her up? Have you used the touch of the hand with a silent or an audible prayer to assuage frenzy, hurry, insecurity? To bring healing to the body? To the spirit?

After you have recovered from sickness, do you want to serve or be served, to take responsibility or be coddled? Does self-pity play a part in your life?

Simon's mother "served them." How do you say, "Thank you"—by words, letter, phone or deeds? Could you render more adequate thanks? How?

9.
THE HEALING TOUCH
OF THE MASTER

Mark 1:32–34

(32) That evening, at sundown, they brought to him all who were sick or possessed with demons. (33) And the whole city was gathered together about the door. (34) And he healed many who were sick with various diseases, and cast out many demons; and he would not permit the demons to speak, because they knew him.

At sundown, the Sabbath was over. People were able to travel and bear burdens without breaking the law.

There is no rest or seclusion for Jesus. To be a Lover is to be ready to be poured out. Jesus lived the words he spoke: "Greater love has no man than this, that a man lay down his life for his friends" (John 15:13). Each healing cost him heavily, an outgoing of love and power.

Jesus could not choose the time and place for his activities. Some of us can have set office hours and at the end of the day close the door and leave for home. The congregation comes to the church at a stated time, not thronging to one's house. Not so with Jesus. Wherever he went multitudes followed him, sought him out. Yet he was ready and willing. While he did not choose the places where he worked, he did choose the attitude with which he faced these unexpected calls for help.

Jesus healed the sick, blessed the children and cast out demons. Today the church is reclaiming its power to heal the sick. Christians, lay and ministerial alike, have increasing faith in a God who heals body, mind and soul —the total person.

The contemporary equivalent of demon possession is wherever sin has an uncontrollable possession of a man. Violent temper, alcoholism, gambling, lust for power or sex, the desire to harm, dominate or kill can master a man so that he has no control over himself, but is held in the grip of his mania. The mania takes many forms, but whenever a man is its slave, he no longer possesses himself; evil does. In Bible times this was called demon possession.

Jesus held power over such possession. The living Christ holds the same power today. "He breaks the power of cancelled sin,/He sets the prisoner free" (Charles Wesley).

Psychiatry can give us much understanding of what mental and moral sicknesses are—how they came to be and why they persist. Let us welcome any and all help. But we need more than understanding and insight. We need the power to change and to put into practice new patterns of behavior. The Christ who cast out demons in Galilee and brought men to sanity two thousand years ago can break the strangle hold of compulsive sin and evil today. Habits of years can be overcome, men can be brought to new life—to be the persons God destined them to be.

A friend of mine was under psychiatric care for years. He was always learning more about himself and more convincing reasons to justify his deep depressions and his excessive hostilities. One day he confessed to God his bitterness toward his parents, asked the forgiveness of his family for his selfish behavior at home. He wrote a letter of detailed apology to his parents (they were both dead) and burned it as we knelt by the fireplace. He told his family that he didn't know how to love them as they deserved, nor could he. But he said, "With God's help I'm going to try." He gave each of his family a hug amid his tears. He was at that moment a released man and on the highroad to life. He has been continuing on the journey ever since.

QUESTIONS

How fortunate you are if you have a good doctor to whom you can go at any time. Do you realize that you have a friend in Jesus Christ to whom you can go any hour, day or night? Do you avail yourself of his friendship? Of his help? Do you wait until matters get to the critical stage? Why not go earlier and more often? Discuss this with a spiritual partner and make discoveries together.

I have known what it is to come home too tired to play a game of checkers or Monopoly with my children, but if one of them started a quarrel I had plenty of energy to discipline him! After you have done a day's work, are you "too tired" to serve and help your fellow men? Discuss the amazing way in which God can give us that extra strength so as to pour out our love (really his love through us) for others. Cite experiences when you have known this to happen.

A doctor in a small group said, "God is telling me that I must stop saying, 'No, not another one!' as a late patient enters the office at the close of a busy, tiring day." Some time later I met him. He said, "God is giving me that extra grace." Recount a similar experience.

As you read verse 34, do you find yourself saying, "Lord, heal me"? Where in body, mind or spirit do you need to be healed? The everlasting arms of God are around you at this moment. The power of Christ to make you whole is there within you. "The healing of his seamless dress/Is by our beds of pain" (John Greenleaf Whittier). Will you claim his healing now and step out in faith as a new person? Will you continue this walk of health and wholeness day by day in the great love of God?

Jesus not only forbade these demons to speak but he frequently commanded those whom he healed to be silent (1:44; 5:43; 7:36). He himself would announce his Messiahship when the time was ripe. Do you tell other people's stories or let them announce their own? Are you so anxious for excitement, to be the bearer of news that you take center stage telling another person's experience, thus depriving him of the joy of telling? Tell of times when you have held back and let another tell his story.

10.
THE WILL TO SAY NO

Mark 1:35–39

(35) And in the morning, a great while before day, he rose and went out to a lonely place, and there he prayed. (36) And Simon and those who were with him followed him, (37) and they found him and said to him, "Every one is searching for you." (38) And he said to them, "Let us go on to the next towns, that I may preach there also; for that is why I came out." (39) And he went throughout all Galilee, preaching in their synagogues and casting out demons.

Verse 35: Jesus had had a busy day on Saturday, but he was up early this Sunday morning. I fear I often sleep late and shorten my devotions after an exhausting day! He who was God's Son and whom we might suppose had less need of prayer found himself in need of renewed strength and fellowship with God. How much more we!

Now that I am retired and do not have as structured and as busy a program as when I was in the pastorate, I find that it is easier to neglect my prayer time. How we tend to neglect the most important friendship in the world!

Verses 36–37: This impulsive Simon who cannot even

let Jesus take time to be alone and pray! He is so proud that his Master is in demand. He wants to be party to helping those who are seeking him and so he breaks in. He was impatient with Jesus' taking time to pray. But later he would be saying, "Lord, teach us to pray" (Luke 11:1). Simon says, "Everyone is searching for you." What words to turn a man's head. How few can stand popularity! But Jesus senses and obeys God's will, refusing to respond to the clamoring crowd.

Verse 38: How different we are from Jesus! I can see myself in that situation. I would be tempted to say, "Oh, Simon, thank you for telling me. Are they really seeking for me like that? I must go to them at once. God is giving me this wonderful opportunity to serve them." Here is this sentimental *me* that I am, wanting to respond to every call for service, to be thought of as necessary to everyone. I tend to be a "yes man"—strong on yes and weak on no. Therefore I often overpromise and spread myself out too thin. My yes will not have meaning unless I can also say no!

Jesus could say no. He heard of Lazarus's sickness and we read, "He stayed two days longer in the place where he was" (John 11:6). I can hear myself saying, "Is Lazarus, my dear friend, sick? Let us go at once, let us hurry, he needs me." What a contrast to this poised and guided Jesus! He said to Simon, "Let us go on to the next towns." He said no to man in order that he could say yes to God.

Verse 39: One feels the sense of appointment in Jesus' itinerary, a kind of quiet but majestic tread of One who keeps step to a different drumbeat. " 'Let us go on . . . that I may preach . . . that is why I came out' . . . he went . . . preaching . . . casting out demons."

QUESTIONS

Verse 35: Does your prayer life go by the board if you are busy or tired? Does the prospect of a heavy day become an excuse to omit prayer or constitute a need for a longer prayer time than usual in order to receive sufficient power and wisdom for the day?

Verses 36–37: Do people interfere with your prayer time? How do you take such an interruption?

Are you flattered by the knowledge that people need you (are "searching for you")? Do you easily say yes to others' requests? Are you the kind that must rush in to take care of every sick person? What difference does it make if those requesting help are your family, close friends, or comparative strangers? Why this difference?

Verse 38: Are you the type that needs to say yes less often and no more frequently? or vice versa? Be specific. What motivates you as you say yes, or no? What does this say about you? What steps are you willing to take to do whatever God is prompting, to say no less and yes more often, or the reverse?

Verse 39: Do you have a sense of appointment? Does the word *disappointment* loom larger than *appointment* in your life?

Written deep in the being of every man is the hidden

purpose of God. Are you discovering and beginning to fulfill his purposes for you?

Do you feel called of God—a sense of appointment—to your job, to your husbandhood, wifehood, fatherhood, motherhood? If you are single, do you feel called to be so? How can you increase this sense of appointment and calling?

11.
TWO MEN—
WILL YOU BE BOTH?

Mark 1:40–45

(40) And a leper came to him beseeching him, and kneeling said to him, "If you will, you can make me clean." (41) Moved with pity, he stretched out his hand and touched him, and said to him, "I will; be clean." (42) And immediately the leprosy left him, and he was made clean. (43) And he sternly charged him, and sent him away at once, (44) and said to him, "See that you say nothing to any one; but go, show yourself to the priest, and offer for your cleansing what Moses commanded, for a proof to the people." (45) But he went out and began to talk freely about it, and to spread the news, so that Jesus could no longer openly enter a town, but was out in the country; and people came to him from every quarter.

What a story this is! Two human hearts: the one hurt, rejected almost without hope; the other overflowing with compassion, courageously breaking with custom, interacting, and healing.

Let us seek to identify with each of these two in turn.

Verse 40: Leprosy in Jesus' day was terminal—death on the installment plan (a good description of sin!). The extremities of the body withered, lacked feeling, became insensitive to touch and pain. And the disease grew, more and more healthy flesh fell prey to the illness.

Because of the dread of this disease and the fear of contagion, lepers were exiled from their homes and communities, and were forced to live in leper colonies, with the stigma of "untouchable," "unclean."

We, too, are lepers often following roads that lead to dead ends, often becoming more and more insensitive. I find how easily I can get used to seeing drunkenness, to hearing of or reading about the body count in war or accidents, to the selfishness and corruption in society and the body politic. Paul writes (Eph. 4:19) of people who become "callous" (Goodspeed), "dead to all feeling" (NEB). Descartes wrote, "I think, therefore I am." Perhaps there is a deeper truth to "I feel, therefore I am." Is our depth of feeling the measure of our aliveness? How easily we grow accustomed to the hurts and loneliness of those nearest to us; often more so than to those far away! How easily we take them for granted! Our feeling level becomes low.

Sin, like leprosy, advances. It must expand by feeding on virgin territory. As lying requires the support of bigger lies, more areas of truth succumb to perversion. Gossipers must embellish and enlarge their stories. Lusting for power knows no limit. Sin has a voracious appetite.

This leper had been rejected, hurt, banished from normal living and relationships with healthy people. Isolation and estrangement with all its temptations was his lot.

Verse 41: The other person in the story is Jesus, a wellspring of compassion and healing, who was not afraid to break custom or discard crippling scripts.

Jesus is not turned off by the man's uncertainty as to his willingness ("If you will, you can . . ."). First of all he feels pity, a stepping stone to compassion; and then the outgoing love of a Man who dares flaunt the law that forbids even approaching much less touching a leper. This sick, lonely man senses the warm touch of a strong, healthy hand! Montefiore, the Jewish scholar, says that he knows of no recorded incident where a priest touched a leper!

So here is Jesus' answer to estrangement and isolation —bridging the gap with outgoing, healing love, regardless of rules or public censure. In an insensitive and callous world God calls us in Christ to a recovery of feeling and concern.

Jesus willed the leper's healing, and commanded wholeness. He restored the man to wholeness and fullness of health.

I have prayed for people with what doctors said was terminal cancer. Some were healed, some were not. It is not for me to say who will be healed and only pray for those. I claim by faith the power of God to heal all. Even those dying do not need to die sick. Our God is a God of wholeness, and Jesus brought this wholeness wherever he went. He is asking us to do the same.

Verse 44: Jesus asked the leper to go to the priest. Here is respect and concern for the Mosaic law and for the priestly institution. How easy it is for those awakened with newness of life to disparage the minister and the pillars of the church and even the institution itself!

QUESTIONS

Verse 40: Is there any "spiritual leprosy" in you? Areas of insensitivity? People of whose hurts and pains you are growing less aware? Whom in your family or on the job are you beginning to take for granted?

Are there in you any deeds, acts, trains of thought or imagination which if continued will lead you along dead-end roads? Is anything in you growing that you really do not want to see growing?

Are you becoming less sensitive to social and political ills? The plight of minorities—American Indians? Blacks? Latin Americans? The urban blight? The hostility between the major political parties? War?

Are you willing to come before God, even as the leper, and to ask for the healing power of Christ to cast out sin and its deadly effects? To claim wholeness both for yourself and for a divided and embittered world? Will you face all known "leprosy" (insensitivity) in yourself? Will you confess it before God and man and let Christ make you whole?

Verse 41: The other person in the story is Jesus. Will you see yourself as an agent of God's love and healing? Are there lonely, estranged and isolated people in your *home,* your *church,* your *community,* this *nation* or *world* to whom you can stretch out a warm strong hand bringing a sense of belonging and wholeness? Dwell awhile on each of those italicized areas and let God speak to you.

Do you believe that God wants you and is choosing you as a channel of his love? Do you insist on always being the leper in this story, forever seeking help, or will you for the most part be the Jesus (God working through you) in this story, bringing health of body, mind and spirit to his other children? In which role do you feel more comfortable? Is it the leper role? If so, what keeps you there all the time? What keeps you from assuming the Jesus role of reconciliation, healing and health-giving power?

Verse 44: Can you combine with a warm evangelical spirit a strong love and honor for the church or institution or nation of today, even with all its weaknesses?

Verse 45: When people in their well-meaning enthusiasm throw barrier after barrier in your way, can you take it, can you still lovingly relate to them? When did this last happen?

12.
WE NEVER SAW ANYTHING LIKE THIS!

Mark 2:1–12

(1) And when he returned to Capernaum after some days, it was reported that he was at home. (2) And many were gathered together, so that there was no longer room for them, not even about the door; and he was preaching the word to them. (3) And they came, bringing to him a paralytic carried by four men. (4) And when they could not get near him because of the crowd, they removed the roof above him; and when they had made an opening, they let down the pallet on which the paralytic lay. (5) And when Jesus saw their faith, he said to the paralytic, "My son, your sins are forgiven." (6) Now some of the scribes were sitting there, questioning in their hearts, (7) "Why does this man speak thus? It is blasphemy! Who can forgive sins but God alone?" (8) And immediately Jesus, perceiving in his spirit that they thus questioned within themselves, said to them, "Why do you question thus in your hearts? (9) Which is easier, to say to the paralytic, 'Your sins are forgiven,' or to say, 'Rise, take up your pallet and walk'? (10) But that you may know that the Son of man has authority on earth to forgive sins"—he said to the paralytic— (11) "I say to you, rise, take up your pallet and go home." (12) And he rose, and immediately took up the pallet and went out before them all; so that they were all amazed and glorified God, saying, "We never saw anything like this!"

Verses 1–2: The interruption came as Jesus was about his accustomed task, "preaching the word." Note how frequently Jesus is interrupted, and how he used these unexpected turns of events as opportunities.

Verse 3: Four men were carrying the paralytic. Life includes bearing and being borne. There are times for receiving, for being loved, for resting back in the everlasting arms and letting God do his work, resting in the love of a human being and letting him carry the load. There are also times for giving, for loving, for bearing the loads of others and being as the arms of God to a brother man. God's wisdom and the intuitions of the Spirit will help us know if we are being carried when we should be bearing the loads of others, or unnecessarily carrying burdens when we should be receiving or delegating help.

Verse 4: How far would you go in breaking with tradition, even to such an extreme as destroying property to bring a man into Jesus' presence? It is one thing to invite a man to go to church with you, another to break up a neighbor's roof, shower the people below with dirt and lumps of dried mortar!

Verse 5: Jesus responds at once to their faith and determination by addressing the paralytic tenderly. "My son." One translation has "My lad." Jesus ministers to the whole man, the paralysis of soul and body. I often ask God to minister to my physical need—the headache, the upset stomach, the attack of virus—and am unwilling to face up to a spiritual cause underlying my disability —overwork, crowded schedule, unwillingness to say no, needless fears, worry, self-absorption. In Jewish thinking the body and soul are inseparable and must be treated together (cf. Ps. 103:3). The movement of the body bears witness to the mood of the soul.

Verses 6–7: The onlookers responded variously, some with condemnation and some with approval. The scribes, with grit in their eyes and dirt on their robes from the open roof, were doubly irritated with this man from Galilee who had challenged their form of belief. To them, adherence to the law was more important than serving one's fellow man. They were not ready for this inward and straightforward dealing with sin. So they sat in judgment. But others were amazed and glorified God! Did they see only the outward miracle, that a paralytic walked, or the greater miracle, that God's love through Jesus healed the invisible sin?

Verse 8: Jesus perceived (had a hunch), that they were accusing him in their hearts. Jesus brought his thoughts out into open dialogue with them. His Spirit enables us, when we feel people's antagonism, not to turn away with repressed critical thoughts but to enter into encounter and dialogue.

Verse 12: As the paralytic was able to handle the pallet on which once he had lain in impotence, so we in Christ can use and be master of what once held us in its power. A highly sensitive person no longer withdraws and nurses hurt feelings but uses the sensitivity to be increasingly aware of the needs of others and of opportunities for service. Ill temper no longer holds us prisoner but, disciplined under Christ, becomes conviction and strength of character.

QUESTIONS

Verses 1–2: Do interruptions throw you off stride? Does a messy house keep you from the main job of loving and serving your family or friends? Do you notice your boy's torn clothes before you see his eager face? Your husband's tardy arrival rather than his weary step? What situations throw you off balance most frequently? What can you do about this?

Verse 3: Do you recognize the dual need both to carry and be carried (cf. Gal. 6:2, 5)? Do you give or receive love more often? How do you feel about this? Is God asking you to be more of a "carrier"? Or to be willing to "be carried" more often? Do you lean on a group of other people or are you responsibly encountering God and bringing his spiritual power to those you meet? Are you a self-starter? Or always in need of others to turn you on? In what ways are you a stretcher-bearer bearing people's burdens? Or do you use all your energies in bearing your own burdens with a sprinkle of self-pity in addition? It took four to carry the pallet. Are you a team worker or an individualist? Do you know how to work with others in loving people, in helping them to come to Christ? Or do you want to do it all alone?

Verse 4: Which side do you take when a good deed is done—criticizing or affirming? Do you shudder to think of people breaking roofs to get people to Jesus? Is property more sacred to us than a person? Is it right to pollute a river in order to make steel or paper?

Verse 5: Jesus is Lord of the total man. Do you observe his laws regarding your physical body as with your spiritual self? Diet, sleep, relaxation, exercise, fresh air? Prayer time, infilling, praise, service? In which area do you need more of the healing touch of Jesus? Are you willing to be a priest to your fellow man as Martin Luther suggests, and receive confession and enable him to receive the forgiveness of God through Jesus Christ? Can you think of ways to do this?

Have you ever been priest to another? Telling a little child who has said he is sorry and has asked God's forgiveness, that he is forgiven? Doing the same for an adult?

Verses 6–7: Do you find yourself critical of people if they are helping someone in a manner contrary to your customary procedure? Are you tempted to think that all people should operate in accordance with your standards of behavior?

Verse 8: Contrary to the way of Jesus, I find I often refuse to speak of my negative thoughts and seek to avoid encounter. Do you do that too? Will you learn, along with me, to be more forthright? In what areas is God suggesting that you do this? When you do have encounter, is it done in love?

Verses 9–11: Jesus ministered to the whole man— body and spirit. Are your prayers for healing directed to the total person? If a loved one of yours is sick are you more anxious that his body be healed or equally concerned that he receive the deeper healing that God makes available through this sickness? Do you bring your faith (and Christ's faith through you) to situations of bodily and spiritual disease (dis-ease) trusting that God is working there and then for wholeness?

Verse 12: Give examples of where God has enabled you to use "that on which once you lay." I used to ask my wife to write the circular letters to my parish. I doubted my abilities and leaned on her. God gradually affirmed me and gave me a sense of worth. Then I wrote my own letters, bringing them to her for further help. Once I was impotent in this regard. Now I move out in power. In what areas do you see this kind of a change in yourself?

13.
"I AM NOT SICK"!

Mark 2:13–17

(13) He went out again beside the sea; and all the crowd gathered about him, and he taught them. (14) And as he passed on, he saw Levi the Son of Alphaeus sitting at the tax office, and he said to him, "Follow me." And he rose and followed him.

(15) And as he sat at table in his house, many tax collectors and sinners were sitting with Jesus and his disciples; for there were many who followed him. (16) And the scribes of the Pharisees, when they saw that he was eating with sinners and tax collectors, said to his disciples, "Why does he eat with tax collectors and sinners?" (17) And when Jesus heard it, he said to them, "Those who are well have no need of a physician, but those who are sick; I came not to call the righteous, but sinners."

Verse 14: Passed on. Again we see that wide-awake alertness. Jesus was alive to all that was going on around him, and that included seeing Levi. Was there a previous acquaintance here? Was the encounter on this occasion more leisurely and expanded than the seemingly abrupt, "Follow me"? We do not know. Levi's response is immediate. It is not merely conceptual—"I believe"; or emotional—"I would so like to be a disciple of yours."

It was translated into action. "He rose and followed." He put his security, his future, his all, on the line. Was he married, did he talk it over with his wife and family? We do not know, we only know he accepted the challenge, left all, and followed Jesus.

As a tax collector in the employ of the hated Roman government Levi was considered an outcast. Everyone put a label on him: "Tax collector." But Jesus saw him as one with a potential for apostleship!

Verse 15: Jesus seemed to have been the eatingest Person! How often his presence graced social occasions. He was equally at home whether eating or fasting, socializing or praying, teaching or healing. What strange table associates these were! Most of them were from the wrong side of the tracks. Tax collectors who worked for Rome were collaborators and therefore anti-Jewish, just as we have thought of Communists as anti-American. Jesus was known as a friend of tax collectors and sinners. Such association was unpatriotic in that day, yet Jesus seemed to be at home with these people and they with him. What an opportunity this was for Jesus' disciples to see the range of their Master's interests and friendships.

In any conversation or social intercourse there is a flow of the dynamic of power. Sometimes I have made hospital calls in the late evening after a tiring day. Visit after visit had drained my vitality. I entered the hospital with little left to give. The dynamic flow was from the patient to me. His weakness and discouragement left me more tired and discouraged. My only solace was, "I did my duty." But how different when I was rested and vigorous so that strength and healing flowed from me to the patient. In Jesus' socializings, whether he was listening or talking, the flow of power and dynamic was always from him to them. They did not mold him, but he so laughed and loved that something of him was left with them.

Verse 16: The remarks of the scribes are all too familiar to us. The implication is, "It would be appropriate for him to eat with religious people, 'good people,' but not with these collaborators and sinners." In other words, guilt by association! Why did they not speak to Jesus directly? Were they afraid? Did they secretly admire him and yet overtly hate him? The clever answer of Jesus completely disarmed them, but it also added to their resentment.

Verse 17: The irony of Jesus' statement was that the scribes to whom the words were directed had no idea that they indeed were the ones who were sick. They assumed that they were "well" and "righteous." Yet in truth the real paralytic was the scribe! But his self-righteousness and blindness kept him from perceiving that he was the one in need of a physician.

How pathetic is the sickness of those who think they are perfect, blind to faults that are so apparent to beholders! The man who, knowing he is sick, comes to the Master is healthier than he realizes. Jesus calls all, but it is those in need, sinners, that respond. When I cease to acknowledge my humanity, my sinfulness and my need, I am deaf to his call and unable to respond. When I think I have arrived and have made it, I think I have little need of the Master. It is then that my spiritual failures occur. It is then that I am truly in need.

QUESTIONS

Verse 13: Do you have favorite haunts, regular times of leisure and refreshment? What is their value? How do you feel when interrupted? Are you in a mood to minister to those who break in on you? *Verse 14:* Jesus may have gone to the sea because he knew people were there. Do you go where people are that you may serve them? Who are the Levis in your community? The people with "labels"? Blacks, people in jail, in a mental hospital, members of the opposite political party or of a church teaching different doctrines from yours? How do you approach them? Are you abrupt? Or is your entry gentle? Is it with a love that cares? This is always a must whatever the method!

Jesus called Levi into discipleship and into a fellowship. Do you accept responsibility for people, nurturing them, helping them to grow? Do you introduce them to a group that will give them supportive fellowship? Talk over the steps that you are taking for some of the people for whose spiritual growth you are accepting responsibility.

Verse 15: What kind of guests do you entertain most often? Churched? Unchurched? Members of minority groups, people that society frowns on? The right kind? Your kind? Those that will return the invitation? Are you comfortable with people from a different background culture and/or with different ethical standards?

Verse 16: Do you talk behind people's backs or go straight to the person concerned when you have a misunderstanding to rectify? Do you whisper innuendoes?

Gossip? Failure to speak directly is often a cop-out. Discuss where you are in this regard.

When socializing with groups in varied situations, is the flow of dynamic from you to them or in the opposite direction? Do they tend to bring you to their level? Or is the conversation such that each is refreshed in mutual fellowship? Do you see just having fun with people as being God's will for you? And equally as important as praying with or witnessing to someone? Can you see it as a witness in and of itself, a prayer lived out in "joy language"?

The scribes were condemning Jesus because of the company he kept—guilt by association. Are you prone to judge people like that?

Verse 17: There were two groups of people here: first, the socially acceptable scribes who were guilty of Pharisaic self-righteousness with their critical condemnation, akin to the attitude of the elder brother in Jesus' parable (Luke 15:11–32); second, the tax gatherers and sinners, socially unacceptable, who were rebellious against the religious and moral standards of their day. One group was sick and did not know it. The other recognized its condition and many sought healing.

Do you see yourself relating in any way to either or both of these groups? None of us is totally healthy. In what way can the Spirit of Jesus, the physician, bring us to fuller health? Does he, on the one hand, cure our blindness so that we see our needs? And on the other, melt our pride and stubbornness that we turn from our known sins?

14.
NO! <u>NEW</u> SKINS

(18) Now John's disciples and the Pharisees were fasting; and people came and said to him, "Why do John's disciples and the disciples of the Pharisees fast, but your disciples do not fast?" (19) And Jesus said to them, "Can the wedding guests fast while the bridegroom is with them? As long as they have the bridegroom with them, they cannot fast. (20) The days will come, when the bridegroom is taken away from them, and then they will fast in that day. (21) No one sews a piece of unshrunk cloth on an old garment; if he does, the patch tears away from it, the new from the old, and a worse tear is made. (22) And no one puts new wine into old wineskins; if he does, the wine will burst the skins, and the wine is lost, and so are the skins; but new wine is for fresh skins."

Verse 18: There are man-made patterns of religious behavior—feasting and fasting, emotional and nonemotional responses, social action and pietism. Our methods of response to God are determined by our childhood, by our culture scripts and by temperament. People accustomed to controlled emotions might feel uncomfortable in a jubilant and victorious funeral service of a black Christian. The forty days of fasting and prayer in the wilderness, and the eating and drinking with publicans and sinners later, would suggest that Jesus was equally at home in either dimension.

Note the strange combination of "John's disciples and the Pharisees" as people who fast. The establishment (the Pharisees) and the radicals (John's followers) were named as being opposed to Jesus' way of teaching. People of different faiths and persuasions often follow similar patterns of behavior though with different motivations. During recent war years Quakers, because of their peace activities, were accused of being Communists! A man can go to church because he wants to praise God or to be with "the right people." He can stay home because of those "hypocrites" or because he is wrestling with honest doubts. How easily we type and judge people, when we know so little about their motives. No wonder Jesus said, "Judge not."

Verses 19–20: There is a time for joy, when the "bridegroom is with them," and a time for sorrow, as when Jesus gave his valedictory the night he was betrayed. One sees in Jesus the capacity to be totally joyous on occasion, and also to know deep sorrow and heartbreak. He embodied his maxim, "Weep with those who weep and rejoice with those who rejoice."

Verses 21–22: It is difficult for some of us oldsters to accept the present-day social and religious revolution. How we have resisted long hair, or the introduction of the guitar and folk music into church services! Some young Christian friends of mine in Manhattan were winning other youth to Christ. They enrolled them into Bible study classes. Sometimes these new converts still relapsed into the use of drugs. They regularly drank heavily and slept with the opposite sex. My puritan training cried out, "Why not tell them they are wrong? Can't they see Jesus forbade these things?" But my friends remarked, "It will mean more to them when the voice comes from within. Let's keep the avenues of communication open and wait for the Holy Spirit to speak to them."

My friends loved these young people, sitting up nights with them as they wrestled "cold turkey" with their addiction. They spent countless hours in fellowship with them. They told of the miracle-working power of Christ and challenged them to become enablers in the recovery of others in their neighborhood. The Holy Spirit spoke during the months and slowly the habits of liquor and promiscuous sex began to disappear. The Word had come from within!

My old wineskin of puritan ethics, with its fixed moral behavior patterns for people has been burst again and again. God has to keep giving me a "stretchable" heart that receives the new, that loves this new breed of Christian and seeks to relate to people as Jesus did.

When Jesus said, "New wine is for fresh skins," he was saying in part, "Learn to accept people, sit where they sit, seek to understand their loneliness, their motives, their longings for meaning and fulfillment." God through Christ can give us new wineskins for old. This is part of the miracle of rebirth.

QUESTIONS

Verse 18: Do you find yourself in strange company as you work to build God's new world? Can you work outside the institutional church to achieve common goals even though the motivation, behavior and beliefs of people are different from yours? In the P.T.A.? On the job? Working for peace? For antipollution? To raise money for the United Way? To help restore a depressed neighborhood? To work for civic justice?

Verses 19–20: Can you give yourself wholeheartedly to joy and to sorrow as occasion demands? Do you "feel good" about being glad or sad? Can you be one with people in their differing moods? What keeps you from really rejoicing? Jealousy? Envy? Stodginess? Wanting to take credit for their joy? A critical thought that their joy will be short-lived? What helps you to rejoice with them? Seeing them as God's children? Praying for them? A withholding of yourself from getting into the picture with your story of greater achievements? Ask yourself similar questions about what helps or what hinders you from "weeping," entering into real empathy with those who weep.

Verses 21–22: How quickly do you adjust to new customs? Behaviors? Methods of worship? New songs? New life styles? New dress styles? Distinguish between some of the things that should be unchanged and those where change is either wise or of no serious consequence. (See Heb. 12:27–29.) Where is the line between flexibility and firmness in your life? Is it changing? In what are you more flexible, in what way more firm? Why? In what ways has your love become more inclusive, embracing others who have behavior patterns and creeds that differ from yours? Have the old wineskins stretched or has God given you a new wineskin? What does *wineskin* stand for in your life? Your faith? Love? Beliefs? Dedication? A framework for security and meaning?

15.
MAN: PAWN OR PERSON?

Mark 2:23–28

(23) One sabbath he was going through the grain-fields; and as they made their way his disciples began to pluck ears of grain. (24) And the Pharisees said to him, "Look, why are they doing what is not lawful on the sabbath?" (25) And he said to them, "Have you never read what David did, when he was in need and was hungry, he and those who were with him: (26) how he entered the house of God, when Abiathar was high priest, and ate the bread of the Presence, which it is not lawful for any but the priests to eat, and also gave it to those who were with him?" (27) And he said to them, "The sabbath was made for man, not man for the sabbath; (28) so the Son of man is lord even of the sabbath."

Verses 23–24: Recently my son and his wife spent a year in Israel and became warm friends with a couple who lived in the apartment below. One Friday evening the couple's young son knocked on the door and said to my son, "My father wants to know if you will let one of your boys come down and light one of our candles. It has gone out." Here was this delightful couple, so human and friendly, and yet bound by the Jewish tradition that to relight a candle is work and therefore breaking the

Sabbath! It was perfectly all right to ask a gentile to do this.

It was traditional that the teachers of the law interpreted the plucking ears of grain as threshing and therefore as breaking the Sabbath. How often our attempts to be religious prevent us from being warm and responsible! I recall, years ago, being so anxious to please and obey God that I continued my morning devotions quite oblivious to the fact that my wife was rushing around with the children, dressing them, getting breakfast while I calmly read and prayed. A man said to me recently, "I see that I have been trying to be so spiritual and so full of good works especially in the church that I have failed to be joyous in my own home." A husband can make habitual TV viewing more important than enjoying his family.

Verses 25–26: Meticulous adherence to rules, rigid fulfillment of program and schedule can easily crowd out the laughter and celebration in life. Jesus points out that David broke a religious law to fulfill a human need. Then he states the principle that the need of a person is of greater importance than observance of Sabbath laws. Let us be sure we interpret *need* not as wants and selfish desires, but as that which is necessary for meaningful growth and fulfillment of personhood.

Verse 27: One can extend this principle to other areas. Marriage is made for man and woman, they are not made for marriage. Business was made for people, not people for business. Sports were made for human beings, not human beings for sports. TV was made for people, and not people for TV. Books were made for us, and not we for books. Yet how often we work so hard at marriage and miss its joy. We give ourselves to earning a living, but not living lives, manipulating and being manipulated, depersonalizing and being depersonalized. The amateur spirit of pleasure and sportsmanship can be bartered for the love of money, the lust for power, for retaliation and even mayhem. Man becomes a pawn in the game. The crowds are spectators removed from the rewards of participation. TV has made slaves of many, determined their life styles, changed and limited social graces, conversation and family activities.

QUESTIONS

Verses 23–24: Contrast the fault-finding, legalistic spirit of the Pharisees with the large, warm and inclusive attitude of Jesus. In which category do you find yourself. Or are you like me—sometimes in one category and sometimes in the other? Talk about this.

Verses 25–26: Cite some instance where you might break religious rules, family customs or church traditions, dress styles, Sunday buying, sitting on the altar rail, divorce, coffee instead of grape juice or wine for the Lord's supper, omitting the church service in order to take care of crops for a sick neighbor, etc. How do you feel about these? What would be the spirit of the Master under these circumstances? Little will be gained by discussing these new patterns of behavior as such. That would cause endless and probably profitless debate. Rather, speak of your experiences as you have been involved in situations such as these. What were your reactions and inner feelings?

Suppose your teenage son was in a track meet which because of heavy rain was postponed to Sunday afternoon. Because of distance you must miss church in order to drive there. What do you do? How do you feel about it?

Verse 26: Think through each of the suggested areas —Sabbath observance, preserving the marriage, attention to business, participation in or the viewing of sports, watching TV, reading. Are you letting any of these rob you of the joy of living, the meaningfulness of life, the warmth and love of the family, the opportunity for the enjoyment of God and his world? Are you becoming enslaved in these areas? Or are these situations and pursuits ministering to you and enhancing your personhood?

16.
CONFRONTATION

(1) Again he entered the synagogue, and a man was there who had a withered hand. (2) And they watched him, to see whether he would heal him on the sabbath, so that they might accuse him. (3) And he said to the man who had the withered hand, "Come here." (4) And he said to them, "Is it lawful on the sabbath to do good or to do harm, to save life or to kill?" But they were silent. (5) And he looked around at them with anger, grieved at their hardness of heart, and said to the man, "Stretch out your hand." He stretched it out, and his hand was restored. (6) The Pharisees went out, and immediately held counsel with the Herodians against him, how to destroy him.

Verse 1: Handicapped people were everywhere, some with visible weaknesses, some with invisible limitations —of body and soul.

Verse 2: How difficult it is to perform when you know you are being watched by critical, hateful people.

Verse 3: In spite of this Jesus went forward with unswerving purpose. He does not pussyfoot, postpone the confrontation, seek to do it secretly after the service. The King James Version uses the bold phrase "Stand forth." Any problem is handled more easily when we single it out and look it squarely in the face.

Verse 4: Jesus brings the issue of healing on the Sabbath into bold relief first by singling the man out and then by sternly addressing his critics. They are silent for they have no answer to give. We have the same question of Sabbath observance which was raised in 2:23–28, but elevated from the material sphere (eating grain in that situation) to that of human relations. Jesus implied that to neglect to do good was actually to do harm, to fail to save life was to kill.

Verse 5: Jesus' reaction was natural and human. He was angry because of the hardness of heart of his accusers and their fanatical bondage to their traditions. Where religion makes man subservient to doctrine and church practice, let us beware. When it enhances his personhood, let us rejoice. Jesus did not vent his anger on the Pharisees with useless cursing but sublimated it by using his powers to heal (see comment on 6:34).

We feel the strength of the Master in his imperative word, "Stretch out your hand." The church in general, and the Christian in particular, often speak too softly, or hold a cowardly silence when people are in bonds. Not so with Jesus! The healing is immediate. Sometimes a healing is gradual, but it is nonetheless a miracle. I have seen both instantaneous and gradual healings. Both are the work of God.

A man's arm was considered a symbol and measure of strength. A withered hand therefore suggested impotence and weakness. Jesus' miracle of healing implies the power of the Son of God to give strength and power to his people—power to change, power to endure, power to overcome!

We are always surrounded by the healing, restoring love of God. Wherever we are, he is there offering himself to us. He is available to bring total healing of body and soul. Nowhere is this healing so fully mediated to us as through the Person of Jesus in history, and the Risen Christ within us today.

Verse 6: We take great risks if we throw ourselves into the task of serving our fellows. After Elijah's victory on Mount Carmel, Jezebel swore vengeance. After this act of mercy by Jesus, the Pharisees and Herodians (ordinarily enemies to each other) joined forces to plot his death.

The opposition to Jesus which commenced in chapter 2 reached ominous proportions as the result of this miracle. The die is cast. From now on Jesus lived under the shadow of the cross as his enemies plotted to destroy him.

QUESTIONS

Verse 1: What is your mood, what are your thoughts, whether in pulpit or pew, as you look over a congregation? Do you see them as people with needs? Do you spend the time before the service begins, or during the offering, lifting up people one by one in prayer?

Verse 2: How well do you function when you are being scrutinized by hostile critics? In baseball a man may come to bat amid spectators' boos, and yet he must still perform. How about our performance in the game of life?

Verse 3: When you face a problem or see someone in

need in a public place surrounded by hostility, do you tend to ignore them? Postpone facing the issue? Hope another will come to the rescue? Get involved? Act with courage? Note the forthrightness of Jesus. What does this say to you?

Are there traditions or inhibitions that keep us today from helping people? In the simple matter of picking up litter, I feel frightfully conspicuous and almost an oddball when picking up a beer can on the street. From stopping our cars to let pedestrians pass to taking the hands of the underprivileged, sick or discouraged, we are so often too busy or have "more important" things to do. Think and speak about this. How much responsibility for others should we accept?

Verse 4: Think through the teaching of Jesus that to fail to do good is to do harm. Mention one or two places where you have so succeeded or failed. What might you have done?

Verse 5: Do you get angry at "man's inhumanity to man"—unsanitary rest homes, inadequate mental hospitals, ghettos, unjust imprisonment? Brutality in some jails? Do you keep informed about these? Do you vent your anger in words merely? What do you do?

Do you claim the healing power of God for yourself and/or for others? It is available through Christ. The touch of a hand given in faith and love has healing power. Do you believe this? When and how do you make use of it?

Verse 6: Do you ever feel critical or resentful when others help people by unorthodox methods?

17.
THE LAITY AT WORK

Mark 3:7–19

(7) Jesus withdrew with his disciples to the sea, and a great multitude from Galilee followed; also from Judea (8) and Jerusalem and Idumea and from beyond the Jordan and from about Tyre and Sidon a great multitude, hearing all that he did, came to him. (9) And he told his disciples to have a boat ready for him because of the crowd, lest they should crush him; (10) for he had healed many, so that all who had diseases pressed upon him to touch him. (11) And whenever the unclean spirits beheld him, they fell down before him and cried out, "You are the Son of God." (12) And he strictly ordered them not to make him known.

(13) And he went up into the hills, and called to him those whom he desired; and they came to him. (14) And he appointed twelve, to be with him, and to be sent out to preach (15) and have authority to cast out demons: (16) Simon whom he surnamed Peter; (17) James the son of Zebedee and John the brother of James, whom he surnamed Boanerges, that is, sons of thunder; (18) Andrew, and Philip, and Bartholomew, and Matthew, and Thomas, and James the son of Alphaeus, and Thaddaeus, and Simon the Cananaean, (19) and Judas Iscariot, who betrayed him.

Verses 7–9: The reason such a multitude thronged to

Jesus is given in the words, "hearing all that he *did.*" A father returned from a church service and was met at home by his wife and son. The wife asked, "What did the minister say?" The boy questioned, "What happened?" The son came nearer the heart of the matter.

Verses 10–11: There are always "happenings" with Jesus present, not only in history, but now as the contemporary risen Christ dwells in us. Sickness disappears in Jesus' presence. Unclean (evil) spirits recognize him and submit to him.

Verse 12: Jesus was not yet ready to have himself announced as the "Son of God." This phrase, as used in the Old Testament, suggested a Messiah who came with worldly glamour and power. Jesus has much teaching to do for he must give a new content to the term *Messiah.* (We will consider this topic in *Power of a New Life* under 8:27–30.)

Verse 13: Luke (6:12) says that Jesus spent all of the previous night in prayer. He spent time in prayer before important events—in the wilderness before entering on his ministry, in Gethsemane before going to Calvary, and now here before choosing his disciples. We can imagine the content and some of the inwardness of this night of prayer. He must have dreamed and planned for his new Kingdom as he brought these men into his Father's presence in his prayer.

Verses 14–19: The number twelve was suggested by the number of the tribes of Israel. As twelve tribes constituted the whole of Israel, so these twelve men would be the beginning of a new Israel, the Kingdom of God. Jesus is not intent on restoring the lost glory of Israel, as we might dream today of restoring the lost power of the Church. His Messiahship is radically different from the popular concept of the Messiah—a mighty king crushing his enemies! The power of Jesus' Kingdom was to be derived from sacrificial love incarnated in himself and in his people. Jesus would show the way and seek to instill this new life style into his disciples.

These twelve men are to learn to live and work in community. Does Jesus deliberately choose men some of whom appear to be poles apart in background, temperament, political leanings? Is the Master setting out to demonstrate that all men, no matter how far apart, can be welded into a fellowship through the great love of God as seen in him, Jesus? Paul writes later, "He . . . has made us . . . one, and has broken down the dividing wall of hostility" (Eph. 2:14).

Let us see the leap of faith in the heart of the Master. He is entrusting the continuation of his Kingdom to these twelve men. Jesus dreamed of ordinary people, laymen taking over, carrying on, doing greater works even than he did (John 14:12).

Finally, he knows he must make a never-ending investment of love in these men, teaching, training, forgiving, with unswerving faith in them. He cared for Judas just as he did for Peter. He loved them all, seeing their potentials, dreaming and hoping for each one day by day. Did Jesus lay his hands on them? (How often he touched people.) Did he have a special word for each? Was there a flash of recognition as their eyes met, one after the other, each man feeling a call, a trust, a new birth?

Verse 14: They were called for three things: to be with him, to be sent out to preach, to cast out demons. They were to become a group of disciples (pupils) enrolled in an informal class, taught and given practical training by their Rabbi, Jesus.

QUESTIONS

Verses 7–9: People thronged to Jesus because they saw something in him. Things happened where he was. Are things happening where you are? This question should not prompt us to get busy using pressure to convince and change people. It should raise questions about the reality and discipline in our life style. Is it self or the Spirit of Christ that shines through? If the latter, happenings are bound to occur in God's good time.

Verses 10–11: Are you successfully marshalling the forces of love, prayer, faith and imagination to do battle against the forces of disease and evil, whether in a human body or the body politic? Speak of some situation where God is nudging you to get into action.

Verse 12: Note Jesus' sense of timing. He was not ready to announce his Messiahship. He was to say, "I have yet many things to say to you, but you cannot bear them now" (John 16:12). Do you find yourself rushing ahead of God? Exploiting situations before they are ripened? Speaking forthrightly to people before building an atmosphere of trust and love? This verse was addressed to evil (unclean) spirits. Is egotism the evil spirit in us that causes us to speak in an untimely, unguarded manner? (See 1:34, 44.)

THE LAITY AT WORK

Verse 13: The busier we are the more we need to pray. Do you find yourself, like me, neglecting prayer life at busy times, when indeed prayers should be increased? What can be done about this?

Verses 14–19: Do we hope to restore ancient glory? To return to the good old days? To see the churches filled again? To recapture the joy of past days? Jesus found he had to walk the pathway of suffering and was called to establish an entirely different kind of a Kingdom —one of sacrificial, self-giving love. What does this say to us about ourselves and our contemporary church? Do we seek for security in old pathways or offer ourselves to blaze new trails in the spirit of him who was the Pioneer of our faith (Heb. 12:2, Moffatt)?

Are we to restore the church as of old or to move forward in the Spirit to new forms and shapes? Do we look for great leaders to rescue us, or do we really see God in the common man, in ourselves? Jesus trusted his message to ordinary people. Can we believe he has so trusted us? How do we feel about this? Can we believe in and trust others even as the living Christ trusts us?

Note the diversity of background and outlook of the disciples. Do we have faith to believe that people poles apart can become one in Christ? That Jesus has and will break down the barriers that separate us? Do we move into every group situation—job, home or church—believing in the ultimate miracle of community?

Jesus' way of life can be summarized in these two sentences: "Greater love has no man than this, that a man lay down his life for his friends" and "He loved them to the end" (John 15:13; 13:1). What does this say to us about the quality of love we give to others? Are

we so loving and living with people that we enable them?
Are we training them to take our places? Or other places
of leadership? Are we producing satellites and "feeders"
or reproducing self-starting, initiating reproducers?

Do you reaffirm each other's place in life from time to
time as fathers, mothers, craftsmen, deacons, pastors?
Have you ever laid hands on another, or clasping a hand
and looking deep into another's eyes reaffirmed someone's parenthood, calling to a profession, to the diaconate,
or to a pastorate?

We, too, are called to be with him, to bear witness
and to do victorious battle with evil. Jesus filled the
word *Messiah* with a deeper meaning. Do we need to fill
such words as *salvation* with a new and deeper meaning?
What does *salvation* mean in the world today with fragmented people, lacking oneness and identity, fragmented
nations with classes and groups snarling at each other?
Liberation? Deliverance? Health? Wholeness? Peace
(*Shalom*)? What part can we play in bringing this kind
of salvation to the world? To our community?

18.
THE CHOICE IS ALWAYS OURS

Mark 3:20–27

Then he went home; (20) and the crowd came together again, so that they could not even eat. (21) And when his friends heard it, they went out to seize him, for they said, "He is beside himself." (22) And the scribes who came down from Jerusalem said, "He is possessed by Beelzebul, and by the prince of demons he casts out the demons." (23) And he called them to him, and said to them in parables, "How can Satan cast out Satan? (24) If a kingdom is divided against itself, that kingdom cannot stand. (25) And if a house is divided against itself, that house will not be able to stand. (26) And if Satan has risen up against himself and is divided, he cannot stand, but is coming to an end. (27) But no one can enter a strong man's house and plunder his goods, unless he first binds the strong man; then indeed he may plunder his house."

Verses 20–22: The opposition described in 2:1–3:6 is resumed here in 3:20–27. If this event followed immediately after the night of prayer and the calling of the disciples, we see once more how temptation and trial come often on the heels of an exalted experience.

Friends describe his actions, "He is beside himself." His enemies impute motives, ". . . by Beelzebul . . .

he casts out demons." We are always on dangerous ground when we diagnose why a person behaves as he does. Let us look to our own motivations however. One can seek to love a mate in order to hold a home together, not because of a joyous love that just bubbles over to one's parner. The motive can be pride. "What will the neighbors think if my marriage goes on the rocks?" "I'll be forever branded a failure if I go through a divorce court." In my own case, I may lead retreats for the selfish joy I get, the love of a sense of power, to gain more skills in the field of group dynamics. Certainly at times these thoughts and desires are peripheral and occasionally get to the center of my thinking. I need then to come back to the central theme of my life: "As Jesus loved and gave himself for me, and as countless people have loved and given themselves for me, so my deepest desire is forever to give of my life for my fellow man."

Verses 23–26: What a keen mind Jesus revealed here! He at once saw the weakness of the scribes' logic as he asks, "How can Satan cast out Satan?" Follow these powerful analogies of the divided kingdom and divided house. True, Satan constantly rises up against himself. Evil has within itself the seeds of its own destruction. Evil, which once entered so enticingly, eventually becomes so ugly and grotesque that we turn away in horror or disgust. But in the meantime it has exacted a frightful toll from those who have embraced it.

Verse 27: Wise is that man who refuses to be bound by evil, so that evil cannot enter his life, and despoil his character. Each man holds the decision as to what thoughts he will entertain, what desires he will foster, what actions he will take. The choice is his. Let him once surrender to evil and an alien spirit has entered his soul and "plunders his goods."

QUESTIONS

Verses 21–22: Do you differentiate between describing a person's actions and assigning motives? When a child, drying the dishes, drops a glass, it is one thing to say, "You were trying to help me and I love you," adding a warm embrace. It is entirely different to say, "You were careless," or "I'll bet you did that because you were angry at having to do the dishes." To impute motives is to move into the realm of judgment which Jesus expressly forbade. Cite some example where you have judged and imputed motives. What might you have done instead?

Verses 23–26: Are we divided personalities, alternately hating and loving? lusting and disciplined? Spendthrifts and stewards? Examine yourself and see the places where you are your own enemy. Speak of these.

The psychologist Fritz Kunkel makes the point that Jesus' words, "Love your enemies," must somehow be applied to us at this point. Can we then understand and accept ourselves as imperfect people with inner conflicts? For my own part, I believe there will be conflicts in some areas of my life as long as I live. If I see someone else wrestling with such a conflict, my heart goes out to him. I lift him up into the stream of God's grace. God understands our battles and is on our side.

We should do this for ourselves. Knowing that God

understands us and loves us as we are, we must also love ourselves. By loving what could be the enemy in us, we turn that enemy into an ally and friend. I used to hate the critical attitudes that swept over me. Now I thank God for a spirit of discernment he has given me. Instead of boxing people in and diminishing them, God is helping me to affirm them, to see their gifts, not their faults, and to rejoice in their growth. An enemy within has become a friend.

Verse 27: You and I, we are the "strong men," but how easily we permit ourselves to be bound with evil. We stand at the gate of our souls, deciding whether to say, "Enter God," or "Enter evil." If the former, it is a loyalty that gives us freedom; if the latter, we become slaves. Talk together of some of the times you have permitted evil to bind you, and of others when you have chosen Christ and God has kept you free.

19.
NO FORGIVENESS UNTIL . . .

Mark 3:28–30
(28) "Truly, I say to you, all sins will be forgiven the sons of men, and whatever blasphemies they utter; (29) but whoever blasphemes against the Holy Spirit never has forgiveness, but is guilty of an eternal sin"— (30) for they had said, "He has an unclean spirit."

I came from England to the United States at fifteen years of age, aided by my mother. My father was angry that I left home and, hoping to maintain his control of me, redoubled his preachments. Every letter urged me to yield my life to the Holy Spirit. Page after page repeated the same message. I dreaded receiving the letters, often left them unopened for weeks and, on reading them, said, "Damn the Holy Spirit." I was angry, vindictive and judgmental. I hated the kind of God he worshiped and I went my own way for years. Finally, in spiritual bankruptcy, I turned to God, repented, and received the Holy Spirit that I had previously damned.

There was neither hope nor forgiveness for me as long as I saw only evil in my Father's concern for me, and as long as I cursed the very Spirit that was to be my salvation. I cannot be forgiven if I deny that which is the hope for forgiveness.

I have on occasion spoken unkindly to my wife. Following that, I may withdraw into my shell and wallow in self-pity and sadistically enjoy the fact that I have hurt her. Later she makes an overture of kindness to me and I think, "So she's unhappy and trying to make up, now let her suffer some more." I impute an evil motive: "She selfishly wants to get rid of her unhappiness." I am not inwardly saying, "She loves me. God help me to love her." If I impute evil motives to another, I cannot receive his forgiveness. Neither can I receive God's if I impute evil motives to him.

The adversaries of Jesus saw what he was doing as the work of evil, for it threatened their position and security. We can be so blind that we do not recognize good when it is at work. Opponents of slavery were called traitors. Pacifists have been called communists. Mankind indeed can become so corrupt that it embraces evil as a way of life. Milton's Satan said, "Evil, be thou my good"! The unforgiveness will go on and on endlessly until I change and begin to see good in God and man. The sin is no longer unforgivable when we change our attitude and start to believe in the goodness of God and look for the good in our fellow men.

QUESTIONS

Have you ever imputed evil to God asking such questions as, "What has God got against me?" "Why is God always picking on me?" These questions bring no satisfactory answers because you assume God to be like man and unfair. But the moment you change your questions to "God, what have you to teach me through this?" or "God, what are you trying to say to me?" then you are imputing goodness to God and the estrangement vanishes and you feel him drawing near.

Do you impute evil motives to people? "TV preachers are in it for the money." "Every politician takes bribes." "My son mowed the lawn for money and not for love." "Your husband gave you that coat to compensate for unfaithfulness." "My pastor is more interested in holding his job than anything else." "People are in ghettoes because they are lazy." "Capitalists are selfish at heart." "Labor unions are a racket." "The Jesus crowd are in it for what they can get out of it." Are there situations where you believe the worst about people, downgrade them and call their motives evil? Think of some, and then realize that to the extent you think this way, *even though it is untrue* that they have these motives, you place a barrier between yourself and them. Forgiveness and reconciliation then become impossible.

What can you do? Start to look for the good in people. Recognize that the traits you condemn in others are already in yourself. Talk out (or write in a letter which you never intend to deliver) your feelings of judgment, and ask forgiveness. God has come to us in Jesus so that we may see the love in the heart of God and also in mankind. To see and believe this is to be on the way to deliverance from any unpardonable sin. Have you had experiences of deliverance in this way?

20.
GOD'S FAMILY

Mark 3:31–35

(31) And his mother and his brothers came; and standing outside they sent to him and called him. (32) And a crowd was sitting about him; and they said to him, "Your mother and your brothers are outside, asking for you." (33) And he replied, "Who are my mother and my brothers?" (34) And looking around on those who sat about him, he said, "Here are my mother and my brothers! (35) Whoever does the will of God is my brother, and sister, and mother."

In the last two verses of this incident Jesus sets forth the spacious reaches of his family. Whoever does God's will belongs in this family. God through Jesus welcomes us into his family. We are to feel at home and to have a sense of belonging. We can claim the fellowship of loving and being loved.

A couple in love find themselves saying, "It seems as though we've always known each other. . . . We're in love for keeps." People in the fellowship of Christ have often, within a matter of hours, found a depth of love beyond understanding. They, too, feel that they have known one another forever, as indeed they have, in the heart of God. As long as they are close to Christ, they continue in this joyous bond of love.

Some of us have come from homes where parents were separated. As a child I often had to listen to disparaging stories from my parents about each other. How meaningful is the family of God where affirmation, listening, trusting and loving are standard procedure!

This family of God is a tie that binds "true hearts everywhere," to use John Oxenham's phrase—little clusters of God's people in a store, a factory, a church, a community. It is at once a spirit reaching out around the world, and showing itself in little inner cores and groups, of deep trusting friendship, heartbeats at the center of institutions secular and sacred alike.

Membership in this family depends on our obedience to God. The Old Testament stresses obeying the Covenant. He is our God, we are his people; therefore we must keep the covenant and obey his laws. The New Testament takes up the theme under the doing of God's will. Jesus said, "I have come . . . not to do my own will, but the will of him who sent me" (John 6:38). "Doing his will" is expressed in the Lord's prayer and the Gethsemane scene. Obedience stands out as a prime demand of God. God's love for us through Jesus Christ is the cardinal truth of Christianity. Our response of loving obedience to his love is the key that unlocks the door to fellowship with God and his family. It is indeed, "Whoever does the will of God is my brother, and sister and mother."

This story is not to be taken as Jesus' rejection of his earthly family. They could well have been concerned about his welfare because of the growing opposition. Their presence could signify their willingness to stand by him. Jesus was not seeking the sentimental or partisan support of his family in an effort to escape trouble. He was calling all (both his natural family and others) who would respond to a new vision of the Kingdom and to obedience to God's will. He was creating the new family of God.

QUESTIONS

Test yourself as a member of God's family. Do you claim a similar quality of fellowship in your spiritual family as in your natural family? Do you feel at home with his children? Are you free to ask help, to claim the fellowship and to believe that others understand? Are you free to help others? And do you feel free to ask help of another?

As you seek to do God's will, do you increasingly feel at home in his world, wherever you may be? Are your spiritual ties in the family of God breaking down all barriers—racial, color, religious, cultural, educational, economic? Take time to think and talk through how real God's family is to you, and how close your brothers and sisters. Does your natural family get pushed aside by your involvement with your spiritual family? Do you find you are avoiding encounter and fellowship at home because it is more difficult to get along with "family"? What is God saying to you about this?

21.
THE STORYTELLER

Mark 4:1–2, 10–13

(1) Again he began to teach beside the sea. And a very large crowd gathered about him, so that he got into a boat and sat in it on the sea; and the whole crowd was beside the sea on the land. (2) And he taught them many things in parables, and in his teaching he said to them . . . .

(10) And when he was alone, those who were about him with the twelve asked him concerning the parables. (11) And he said to them, "To you has been given the secret of the kingdom of God, but for those outside everything is in parables; (12) so that they may indeed see but not perceive, and may indeed hear but not understand; lest they should turn again, and be forgiven." (13) And he said to them, "Do you not understand this parable? How then will you understand all the parables?"

For our study of the section 4:1–20 we will break up the natural sequence, placing in juxtaposition parts of the story with parts of Jesus' explanation. First we will deal with parables in general, following with studies of each of the four kinds of soil.

Verse 1: Picture in your mind this pastoral scene: Jesus sitting in a boat, crowds on the shore, neighboring hills with rocky ledges and stretches of fertile land where a peasant sows his seed as he strides across the field. This is an ordinary situation which Jesus uses to tell a story with extraordinary overtones.

Verse 2: Jesus saw life as parable. To him a little bird recalled the Father's love, a woman making bread acted out the growth of the Kingdom, buried treasure suggested eternal riches.

It is a wise teacher who wraps truth in story form. The hearers may not yet be ready to perceive the hidden truth, but the story is recalled from time to time and at some unsuspecting moment its meaning breaks through with the joy and freshness of discovery.

Verses 10–13: The text refers to two groups of people: The disciples who have "been given the secret"; "those outside" who do not perceive. The degree of perception and understanding is determined by the attitude of the hearer. One must approach life with awe and wonder in order to hear its voice. To understand nature's inner secrets, a person needs to "stand under" its various scenes. Humility and teachableness open the gates to deeper appreciation and understanding.

We become disciples who have been "given the secret" when we stand on the ocean's shore and hum, "There's a wideness in God's mercy like the wideness of the sea," when we see the flight of wild geese and feel something stir deep within us, or when we look up at a skyscraper and stand in awe of man's creation. Life speaks a varied language when we see "sermons in stones and books in running brooks," as Shakespeare wrote.

QUESTIONS

To what extent are you exploring the use of the story form? Do you teach your children more by precept or story? If you teach, Sunday or weekday, is storytelling standard procedure? Can you tell a story without moralizing and let the hearer discover its meaning in his own time? Are you cultivating perception of spiritual overtones in others? Asking children what they feel when they see the ocean, a mountain, a tall tree, a leaping deer, an unfolding flower?

What tends to produce boredom with life so that its vicissitudes reveal no deeper meanings? On the other hand, how may we discover the hidden overtones of life that bring insight and imagination? Tell how you are developing childlike wonder and surprise, the listening ear, the seeing eye.

22.
THE PARABLE OF THE SOILS
A. THE HARDENED PATHWAY

Mark 4:3–4, 14–15

(3) "Listen! A sower went out to sow. (4) And as he sowed, some seed fell along the path, and the birds came and devoured it.

". . . (14) The sower sows the word. (15) And these are the ones along the path, where the word is sown; when they hear, Satan immediately comes and takes away the word which is sown in them."

In this parable the sower represents God moving into human hearts sowing his word. The type of soil where the word falls is the condition of man who must always decide whether and how to receive this word. This is what the Bible is all about: God's endless love and man's response—or, tragically, his lack of response.

The four types of soil are indicative of the various responses that a person may make to God. They also suggest the forms of response that people may make to us. The first three speak to us through a negative approach; the fourth—the good soil—affirms us as it describes the responsive Christian.

Verses 3–4: The wayside, trodden down and hardened by traffic, rejects the seed. *Verses 14–15:* There are areas in all of our lives where we refuse to admit flashes of insight—luminous thoughts, words of warning. Our lives become hardened, and as habit patterns control us we become insensitive to people and situations. Cries of need and the loneliness of human hearts escape us. We shut out the pain of the world. We can close our eyes to new light, new truth, and new ways of doing things. The Pharisee had hardened his heart. His pattern of living was fixed and he received little that was new.

Satan immediately comes and takes away the word. But he would not have an opportunity to do so if we had received the word and acted on it. We laugh when Flip Wilson says, "The devil made me do it," but only because we see ourselves in his remark. Our failure to accept new leadings and growth is often followed by our finding excuses for our sterility and locked-in behavior.

QUESTIONS

The seed is the word. What do you mean by God's word? The words in the Bible? The inner hunches or leadings that come at unexpected times? The recognition of loneliness or need in someone at home, on the job, in church? The urge to write to your Congressman about legislation that seems in line with or contrary to the spirit of Jesus? Think over different ways in which God speaks to you. What discoveries of God's word and will in traditional places such as Bible reading, church worship, times of prayer come to your mind?

What do you hear and see of God's word and will in less traditional ways such as nature, music, art, a human encounter, national and world events?

In what ways recently have you responded to God's promptings? Relive one such instance in your imagination.

What, basically, is the reason (or reasons) why you sometimes refuse to respond? Is it stubbornness, habit, unwillingness to have your comfort disturbed, inertia, prejudice against the place or persons whence ideas or suggestions come? Share these discoveries with someone close to you and think what you can do about this.

Have you noticed that willingness to listen and to respond to God's promptings heightens your sensitivity to his will and makes keen the cutting edge of obedience? Speak of this as well as of the reverse process.

23.
THE PARABLE OF THE SOILS
B. STAYING POWER

Mark 4:5–6, 16–17

(5) "Other seed fell on rocky ground, where it had not much soil, and immediately it sprang up, since it had no depth of soil; (6) and when the sun rose it was scorched, and since it had no root it withered away.

". . . (16) And these in like manner are the ones sown upon rocky ground, who, when they hear the word, immediately receive it with joy; (17) and they have no root in themselves, but endure for a while; then, when tribulation or persecution arises on account of the word, immediately they fall away."

Verses 5–6: Much of Israel's land is rocky ledge, sparsely covered with shallow soil permitting no depth of root. As the hot sun scorches and withers newly sprouting seed, so, Jesus said, tribulation and persecution cause the new Christian to fall away.

Verses 16–17: A student who had committed his life to Christ and had given up drugs said, "You have no idea how hard the fellows make it for you if you suddenly decide to kick the habit." Sometimes we have a moving religious experience, or all at once we determine to start again. We are all fired up, raring to go. Then we encounter the familiar environment with its conflicts and temptations. And we slip! We nod our heads in agreement with the sermon we hear, or a book we are reading, but the pressures of public opinion, or the emotional cost of perseverance are too much for us.

QUESTIONS

Give an example of "staying power" (v. 17, NEB) in your life recently. What is it in you that wants to carry on in spite of opposition or persecution? Are there places where you wilt under criticism? How well do you carry through with your plans? Dieting? Keeping promises? Completing tasks?

In Mark's day martyrdom threatened the church and caused some Christians to weaken. What are the counter-parts of this today? Ridicule? Public opinion? Unwillingness to be different from one's peers? What is most apt to deflect you from your purpose? What do you feel God wants you to do about it?

24.
THE PARABLE OF THE SOILS
C. THE STRANGLERS

Mark 4:7, 18–19

(7) "Other seed fell among thorns and the thorns grew up and choked it, and it yielded no grain.

". . . (18) And others are the ones sown among thorns; they are those who hear the word, (19) but the cares of the world, and the delight in riches, and the desire for other things, enter in and choke the word, and it proves unfruitful."

Verses 18–19: "Worldly cares and the false glamour of wealth and all kinds of evil desire come in and choke the word" (v. 19, NEB). Three things are necessary to ward off these three stranglers of cares, wealth, and evil desires—commitment, a sense of priorities and a continuing awareness of God.

I recall attending a circus where an acrobat stood on two horses, one foot on each. He pirouetted, did somersaults forward and backward. I came home to the farm and hitched two old horses together in an attempt to imitate this feat. But alas! No sooner did I say "Giddyup" than the horses moved forward in diverging paths and I fell, humiliated, between them. One foot on each horse may be good circus technique but it is a disastrous way of life. "Both feet must be on the same horse."

Paul writes, "I want you always to see clearly the difference between right and wrong" (Phil. 1:10, LB). The false glamour of wealth and evil desires lie in wait for us all. How often we can settle for substitutionary successes rather than the costly but rewarding obedience to his will! The secret of resisting the choking effect of these "thorns" is to ensure a vigorous growth of that which is good. The ingredients of a strong healthy inner life are the habits of praise and thanksgiving, a consciousness of God's approval, a feeling of inner worth with its resulting sense of freedom.

QUESTIONS

Do you, like the circus rider, try to put one foot on each horse? Trying to hold on to some of the pleasures of the world fearing that you will not have quite as much fun in the Kingdom?

Have you made an inventory of your commitment to the lordship of Christ? Is he guiding your decisions when you buy a new car, attend a show, cast a ballot, choose from a menu, watch TV, drive your car, talk about your neighbors? Are you more eager for the approval of others than for a sense of inner integrity? Does the desire for personal pleasure take precedence over serving one's fellows? Is the desire for material wealth stronger than the hunger for the treasures of the spirit?

What effect does the constant bombardment of TV ads have on you? The pressures to buy luxuries, comforts, beauty aids?

25.
THE PARABLE OF THE SOILS
D. ROOTED AND GROWING

Mark 4:8–9, 20
(8) "And other seeds fell into good soil and brought
forth grain, growing up and increasing and yielding
thirtyfold and sixtyfold and a hundredfold." (9) And he
said, "He who has ears to hear, let him hear."
". . . (20) But those that were sown upon the good soil
are the ones who hear the word and accept it and bear
fruit, thirtyfold and sixtyfold and a hundredfold."

The good soil bespeaks the response of a joyous and
free man. This man is willing to learn—he hears and
accepts. "Blessed are the meek," i.e., "Blessed are the
teachable." It is not merely to embark on a new pattern of outward behavior, but so to receive the word that
it becomes a part of ourselves and we become new beings.
In the ritual for the sacrament of the Lord's supper or
communion service we read, "Eat my flesh, drink my
blood." This suggests the *inwardness* of the act. There
is a new center of living. We are "good soil" when we are
aware, alive and open to God on every side.

We hear his word in Scripture and in the lives and
words of those in our own homes, school, business. We
hear the word from the Holy Spirit in our inner promptings and hunches. We see him as a part of every experi-

ence from the smile of a little baby to the happenings of the era in which we live.

The hearing and accepting of the word implies that as a seed falls into the earth, dies and becomes the source of new and abundant life, so God's word comes deeply into our lives. We then die to self and self-will; we come alive to God through Christ and become new beings in him.

As a minister I have known what it is like to read my Bible primarily to have material to preach and teach. It came as far as my mind and lips. I discovered ideas, doctrines and principles to be relayed to others. It was a great day in my life when I saw that the words and truths of the Book must penetrate my inner being, even as seed goes deep into the soil and sends forth roots. Even so must I produce roots of honesty, repentance and dedication. This brought a new experience of God and I began to live in a new life style. My preaching was no longer an "idea-lip" message but the story of sin forgiven, of new personal discoveries and joys in him. There were new roots of growth and development witnessing to a changed life and new fruitage.

The growth process is all-important. Jesus' teachings were not given to make us perfect to give us a consciousness of arrival or attainment. Rather they call us to the kind of continued commitment and abandon that fosters growth. There is to be a continuous letting go of the past as we reach to the future. The seed dies that other, new seed, may come into being. This constant dying to live, losing to find, letting go the old to appropriate the new is the growth process Jesus intended. There is a real sense in which we never fully arrive, we are always growing.

QUESTIONS

Do you accept God's word deep within yourself? Or is it a surface obedience? For instance, as a mother, do you more or less dutifully go through the tasks of motherhood or do you have a deep sense of being called by God to motherhood? Are you "stuck" with "those kids" or do you daily choose to be the parent of those wonderful children God has given to you so that everything tends to be done in joy and gratitude? Think of this in relationship to your job, neighbor, school, husbandhood, wifehood, single state, etc. Have you accepted your situation as God's appointment for you? Do you have a sense of joy and rightness in what you are and are doing?

Is your life bearing fruit? Check it by the fruit of the Spirit in Galatians 5:22–23. In what particular situations in life are you apt to fall short in any of these areas? In which of these do you need to grow?

Do you see the "dying-living" process at work in yourself? When you forego your own selfish plans in order to respond to a neighbor's need? Refrain from fault-finding in order to affirm someone? Deny indulgent thoughts to make room for the creative use of your imagination? What other situations of "dying-living" come to mind?

Whenever a part of one's self dies in order that something better may live, we are moving in the Calvary-Easter sequence. Speak of this growth process in your life.

26.
LAMPS ARE FOR SHINING

Mark 4:21–22
(21) And he said to them, "Is a lamp brought in to be put under a bushel, or under a bed, and not on a stand? (22) For there is nothing hid, except to be made manifest; nor is anything secret, except to come to light."

One does not extinguish a lamp as soon as it is lighted. It is put on a stand so that its light may be seen. So also God's light, Jesus Christ, cannot be extinguished. The sun of righteousness will shine forth. The truth of God will not remain hidden, but will be proclaimed throughout the world.

These words underscore Jesus' teachings regarding parables. Parables are meant to be understood. Their inner (hidden) meanings will come to light and become effective in men's lives. God's ways, like parables, seem mysterious. But we will yet see the purpose and plan of his doings.

God's love is given to us, not to be hidden, but to be passed on to others. As naturally as light shines, so his love through us should flow out towards our fellow being. Love should never be a matter of duty, force-fed, but springing up from within like an artesian well.

These verses are a call to faith: God is light and his

light will yet shine in this dark and confused world. His purposes are unfolding. Believe also that his light is shining through you and that it will achieve his purposes. Every deed of unselfish love will bring its reward. The years of parental caring, of faithful service, of joyous input into life will not be wasted. There is nothing lost in the economy of God. His promises are sure. The light and love that have shone through you will accomplish his purposes.

QUESTIONS

Jesus was saying, in effect, "God has chosen that his light should shine through me. This light will not be extinguished, his light and love will go on being revealed and manifested to all of mankind." God's light, though temporarily hidden, will ultimately shine; his love, though often opposed, will ultimately triumph.

Speak of your faith in the ultimate triumph of God in various situations: in history and contemporary events; in your life; in recent years or recent days; in the life of someone you know with a terminal illness; in some specific situation in the current scene where evil seems temporarily to have the upper hand.

Speak of the way in which God's hidden truths come to light for you: the truth in biblical parables; the mysterious workings of God in your life now being made meaningful. Speak of how the hidden purposes of God in past sufferings or reverses are now coming to light and being filled with meaning.

Do you find yourself believing or doubting that the years of your living and loving will be used of God to accomplish his purposes? In what way? Have you thought of yourself as God's lamp? Made by him to shine? To bring light to the lives of others? So to shine that you bring brightness and joy, not gloom or confusion, to people? Do you speak of yourself as a lamp of God? In what way is God being revealed through you?

27.
COMPOUNDED INTEREST

Mark 4:23–25

(23) "If any man has ears to hear, let him hear." (24) And he said to them, "Take heed what you hear; the measure you give will be the measure you get, and still more will be given you. (25) For to him who has will more be given; and from him who has not, even what he has will be taken away."

Verse 23: We can hear mere words, or we can perceive a hidden meaning. Jesus used parables to train people to search for this deeper meaning. He used such words as *water, bread, sheep, leaven* to convey spiritual truths. The Christian seeks to bring a perceptive mind to life's situations.

I recall that after I had been married about two years, my wife said to me, "You don't tell me you love me as often as you used to when we were dating." I *heard* her words, but I did not *perceive* what she was really saying. What I heard were the audible words and my inner reaction was, "So you aren't satisfied with what I do, and you are trying to tell me what I should do. I'm not going to let you run my life." Out loud I said, "Well, I married you, didn't I? You haven't missed any meals."

What a cop-out this was! What a failure to perceive

where she was hurting! What a failure to enter into meaningful dialogue! Underneath those words her heart was saying, "I'm a little lonely today. I'd like so much to hear you say you love me. My folks made so much of me at home. No, don't get me wrong, I don't want to go back to them. I love you and always will, but I'd love to be told that I'm tops in your book. I'd like to be cherished a little." I realize now how completely deaf I was to what she was really saying. I had ears, but I did not hear.

Verses 24–25: Simon Peter's friends must have been amazed when Jesus changed his name from Simon to Peter, a "rock." To them he seemed to be an unstable, impulsive, blundering and thoroughly unreliable man. But what Jesus saw in Simon was determined in large measure by the fact that Jesus looked at him with a love that believed in him and saw a deep potential behind his impulsive actions. That was true of his estimate of every person he met. What he saw in people was what he chose to see. It was determined by the spirit, the understanding and the insight he brought to each person.

In 1930 when my wife and I were planning a trip to Europe we decided to attend that Passion Play in Oberammergau. We spent months reading the play, studying the history of the village and the lore of the region. Imagine our astonishment to hear some of our fellow travelers remark, "I didn't know they would speak in German!"

The more we brought to the play, the more we received and still more was added as we reflected on it. Whereas the travelers who discovered that the play was given in German were disgusted and in no mood to receive the uplift that, despite the language barrier, the acting alone might have given them. "Even what they had was taken away!"

"Take heed what you hear." We could well add, "Take heed what you read and see." We often can choose whether we will hear, read or see bad news—gossip, failure and violence; or, on the other hand, good news— stories of kindness, enterprise and the hazarding of lives for worthy ends. The final test is not what I see and hear but what I appropriate and what it does to me.

QUESTIONS

In the following questions about this text, let us note their connection with Mark's words on understanding parables and the sin against the Holy Spirit (4:10–13).

Jesus places the responsibility for perceptive hearing squarely on our shoulders. The Pharisees would not hear him. They saw no good in him. It was not God but Satan that performed the many acts of kindness.

Think of areas in which God is working and speaking: Russia's rebellion against the tyranny of the Czars and a corrupt church; the growing opposition to war; the rebellion against an establishment (whether church or state) that has been slow to come to grips with the social evils of our time: poverty, racism, pollution, increasing armaments. Do you see God at work here? In what way?

If you see only evil at work in the world, this is a sin

against the Holy Spirit. Faith is believing that God is at work: in the world, in your business, your community, your church and your home. Speak of this. Tell of places where you see your Heavenly Father at work.

Tell of places where you have set out to look for God in events, in nature or in people and as a result you have been blessed with an overflowing of his presence. "To him who has, more will be given." You found so much more than you expected!

Likewise, think of when you looked for negative things in life or people and the little faith you had was taken away!

Do you naturally see the good, the God, in people? Are there some people in your life to whom you frequently react negatively? What is God saying to you about this?

28.
INNER PEACE

Mark 4:26–29

(26) And he said, "The kingdom of God is as if a man should scatter seed upon the ground, (27) and should sleep and rise night and day, and the seed should sprout and grow, he knows not how. (28) The earth produces of itself, first the blade, then the ear, then the full grain in the ear. (29) But when the grain is ripe, at once he puts in the sickle, because the harvest has come."

The man in this parable can sleep at night; he is at peace with himself. He has let God apportion the division of labor. His is to sow and to harvest. He knows that God causes the seed to grow, even though "he has no idea how it happens" (Phillips). He trusts the faithfulness of God. He could well say each night, "There's no need for two of us to stay awake tonight, Lord!" There is an inevitability about the growth of the seed and the ripening of the grain. There is an orderly process in the universe. These words of Jesus are for these people who continually worry about the outcome of their endeavors and who fail to realize that their efforts are not theirs alone.

A major issue of our time is a tendency to strive for

results. We draw up plans, form organizations because of a compulsive drive for success. Jesus, in effect, is saying, "God is your unseen Senior Partner working with and through you. Believe that my Father's Kingdom is coming. The end is in the beginning. Let your light shine. Don't use pressure tactics. 'Let it happen.' Trust my Father to do his part and bring the increase. Your part is to be obedient to God's will and to live a life overflowing with his love. God will do the rest."

QUESTIONS

Do you sleep well nights, knowing that God is at work for you while you rest?

Tell of how, when you have done your best, you rely on the faithfulness of God. What do you do when the worries and anxieties creep in? Recall an instance where you sensed the division of labor: you obeyed God's will and he came through with the results. Are you patient and willing to wait for God's timing? I am often like the little boy who kept pulling up the beans to see how they were doing!

There is an advertising slogan: "You can be *sure* if it's Westinghouse!" How much more sure you can be since it's God! Paul writes, "Of one thing I am certain: the one who started the good work in you will bring it to completion . . ." (Phil. 1:6, NEB).

Do you believe God is at work in you? Will you commit to him your imperfect acts, daily, and trust him to work out his perfect will in and through you? In everything "God works for good with those who love him" (Rom. 8:28).

In addition, the attitude of trust in the growth processes of God should influence our relationship with others. Can you witness to someone and let the matter rest without probing for results? Will you trust the seed to grow? Can you let an adolescent try his wings, blow hot and cold, and know that God is at work there? Can you let him learn from his own mistakes? When in any relationship, you sincerely seek to obey God's will in love, will you believe that God enters in, takes up the slack, and accomplishes his purposes?

29.
THE MIRACLE OF GROWTH

Mark 4:30–32

(30) And he said, "With what can we compare the kingdom of God, or what parable shall we use for it? (31) It is like a grain of mustard seed, which, when sown upon the ground, is the smallest of all the seeds on earth; (32) yet when it is sown it grows up and becomes the greatest of all shrubs, and puts forth large branches, so that the birds of the air can make nests in its shade."

Verses 30–32: The things of the Kingdom start small —Jesus in a manger, Luther standing alone against the whole of Christendom, or William Penn with Bible in hand walking unprotected among the Algonquin Indians.

It was a small thing Sid Martin did. Halfway through a weekend retreat he said to me, "I must go home and see my eight-year-old son. My wife and I have been leaving him alone too much lately, and I've been learning a few things here. Suddenly I'm lonely for that boy of mine." Seeing him go, someone said "You're going to check on that boy of yours?" "Not exactly," he replied. "I guess I need him and he needs me."

He found that through a misunderstanding, the neighbors with whom his son was to stay were away. The boy was home, lonely and frightened. His eyes lit up as he saw his father and then timidly he said, "Are you staying home?"

"Yes, I'm here for the rest of the afternoon and evening to do what you want to do."

The boy's joy knew no bounds.

The next morning when Sid returned to the conference, he showed telltale marks of glue on his fingers. They had built a model airplane together.

What a small thing to do! Building a model airplane with an eight-year-old! But it was more than that. It was rather building a loving and confident relationship. Who can foretell the results?

The Kingdom begins in little kindly acts, in unheralded deeds, the nod of the head, the gracious moving over in a church pew to make room for a latecomer. How small the beginning—how marvelous the way God takes our little and creates his much!

This parable continues the thought of verses 23–29. The growth of the grain is a mystery ("he knows not how," v. 27). The growth of the mustard seed is likewise a mystery. The great mystery of life is how God's Spirit helps small beginnings become mighty acts and evidences of this invincible power.

QUESTIONS

Verses 30–32: Recall a small beginning of something that is now so important, even wonderful, in your life!

Are you the type that is willing to "start small" and let God bring growth? What does this say about you?

The nesting birds found protection in the branches. How do people find reassurance, take new heart, because of you? Do you see yourself as someone whose priority is to take care of yourself and your possessions ("If you don't look after yourself, no one else will"!), or as someone who has become "a person for others"? Talk of this.

Think of this tree as a place where under its branches you find protection and refuge in the love of God. What is this saying to you? Think also of your life as a tree that protects and shelters others. What is this saying to you? About your own need of growth and maturity so as to provide better shelter for others? Your rootage in the God who shelters and protects us all? The use of your growth for service and protection of others rather than growth for bigness or security's sake or for personal satisfaction?

30.
BUILDING A GROUP OF RESPONDERS

Mark 4:33–34

(33) With many such parables he spoke the word to them, as they were able to hear it; (34) he did not speak to them without a parable, but privately to his own disciples he explained everything.

Verses 33–34: The use of parables attested to both the wisdom and the skill of Jesus. Many people would have rejected his teaching if he spoke openly of his Messiahship and his way of life. They would have refused to enlist as members of his Kingdom if he had made an obvious appeal. His parables, drawn from incidents in their daily lives, were apparently harmless and nonprovocative. They were not rejected but received and retained. Once in the minds of the listeners these parables began to work like leaven unfolding their truths. People thought about them. God's spirit worked in people's minds. People recognized truths without realizing whence they came. It was as though folks discovered them for themselves!

The parable form tends to make the hearer think for himself. Often in his less conscious moments, ideas come with a sense of discovery and illumination. What was only heard at first is now perceived. It is like looking at an Impressionist painting where innumerable dabs of yellow and blue are placed in close proximity. The viewer sees these two primary colors and unconsciously mixes them himself in his mind's eye, and the resultant green has an unbelievable aliveness to it. So the truth often leaps out with a living reality, because the hearer has himself suddenly discovered the meaning of the parable—even though it be years later!

The disciples, who are committed followers, are ready to be taught. They will receive the truths of the parables without opposition. The general public would not.

QUESTIONS

The parable or story form gives data rather than conclusions. Its use helps people think and discover for themselves. It avoids pressuring people to come to quick and premature decisions. As a friend, parent, teacher or leader, how do you rate yourself? More apt to furnish data than conclusions and let people do their own thinking? Able to live with incompleted situations and slowly developing people rather than forcing premature decision on them? Do you see yourself more as an enabler helping people discover God's will rather than an adviser and maker of decisions for people?

Think about the phrase, "As they were able to hear it." Babes need milk; adults require sturdier food. Do you continue with childish prayers and teachings when mature approaches are indicated? Do you ever come on too strong? God mercifully did not reveal all my sins to me at once. He knew I could not have taken it! Do you tailor your material and your approaches to the needs of people in various age groups or in different stages of religious development? Give examples of success and/or failure in this.

Jesus loved all people, but he spent by far most of his time with those who responded to his message. His hope for the growth of the Kingdom lay in concentrating his energies on the few. What is your strategy? Trying to get everybody to respond, or scattering the seed with a love for all but building in deeply with the few?

Do you, like Jesus with his disciples, give yourself unreservedly to the smaller group of responders in order that they in turn may take initiative and become "communicators of life"?

CONCLUSION

In these first four chapters of Mark, Jesus has become very real to us. He was a human being; tempted as we are, meeting criticism and opposition. The thrust of his life was to bring wholeness to body and spirit. He has gathered around him kindred spirits, to whom he will trust his enterprise, the Kingdom of God. He was more than man—he was God become flesh, God's power and love made available to us. He introduced us to a new life style, one of amazing openness and honesty, one of deep, caring love. He was God's man, but also our man, as he demonstrates this way of life and makes it available for us. At every turn we feel the hope and empowerment he has brought to us.

The next volume, *Power of a New Life,* will deal with who this Jesus was, and the nature of his mission. We see him in his humanity, and yet as one who possessed the majesty of the Son of God. The opposition with the Pharisees heightens. Life moves inexorably to a tragic conclusion. How does he prepare for this? What is his mission? Why must he so radically change the old Jewish concept of the Messiah? How does he face this mounting opposition?